12·16·18

FIVE MILES DOWN A SIX MILE ROAD

Thomas R. Ruffin

FIRST EDITION

ISBN-13:978-1523724000
ISBN-10:1523724005

cover art and design – Steve H. Cash
back cover photograph – Nikki Hall

Karma Goat Press
Clinton, Mississippi

Karma Goat Press
Clinton, Mississippi
United States of America

Printed in the United States of America

1 2 3 4 5 6 7 8 9 0

ALSO BY THOMAS R. RUFFIN

On The Weeping Floor

Sideways Train

The Mudhole Collection

The Empty

Black Church

The Precious Indignity

The Idiocy of Sara

CONTENT

for those that believed in me
… when I didn't believe in myself

To Begin With

For many people poetry means nothing at all. It carries no weight of import on their lives and has no discernable impact on their day to day disposition. For others, though, poetry is everything, it is their life. It is what sustains them. Some claim poetry to be their salvation. Somewhere in between is where most of us find ourselves with regard to the role that poetry has in our lives

There are many mythical perceptions and beliefs about poetry ... and those that write it, yet there are only but a handful of its' characteristics, value and behaviors that are found to be universally true:

There is, I believe, a mistaken underlying notion that poetry is to be beautiful and exude a tone of whimsicality and positive energy; and/or that poetry should look like this or that and sound like that or this. Not so ... In fact ... I, being no scholar of poetry and having no authority to do so ... am announcing to the world that there are no rules with regards to poetry.

Poetry should be, in an individual context, what we desire it to be. I am concerned for the sanity of those that attempt to grasp it, hold it, study it, measure it, dissect it and somehow ... define it.

It is my assertion that poetry should be as free as the air ... to move about and to visit us when it cares to do so. It should not be owned ... it should be as a gift, whether written or read ... a gift that is given with no expectations of reciprocation.

Poetry is words, together and alone, that are written in an effort to describe those things ... those things, that at some point, we will learn ... cannot be described.

In my way of thinking poetry is to be enjoyed much as a cooling breeze might gently yet chaotically dance by kissing the nape of the neck softly on a particularly humid summer afternoon. Or upon the recognition of a once familiar fragrance, the origin being unknown.

The writing of poetry has little to do with form or the proper alignment of words or evenly distributed stanzas that appear uniform to the page and quite well behaved. It has even less to do with how it fits into any of a great number of categorical boxes given silly names by ... man.

In my estimation poetry is either to be gotten along with or not. Like a neighbor that comes around on some days to converse in congenial manner and on the day after he is as ill-tempered as a displaced hornet.

No one man or any group of mankind should be allowed to deliver commentary of worthiness or value to any words of poetry not written by themselves. The value of a poem is immeasurable. To some it might be worth a cavern of gold ... to others no more than a copper penny. But, no man possesses such authority, or wisdom, to assign to poetry a mark of worth.

Poetry is passion in written form. It is emotion represented by marks on a page. It is pseudo physical lettings of the heart. It is the rendering of meadows, mountains, streams and oceans and their intertwined relationships ... by not the brush of paint but by the color of words.

Poetry, at best, is healing and cathartic of mind. Often though, it is the unadulterated truth ... possibly on a deeper level than we are able to comprehend ... it is what is not owed to us ... it is the truth explained.

Poetry is the revealing and illuminating of evil ... the essence of life. It is our spiritual birth ... it is from where we come.

Poetry is a sun burdened gravel road that winds its way through and past the lives of the downtrodden. It comes from within and often ... it comes by the force of great emotional conflict.

Poetry is the indescribable. It can come to us as a warm, soft breath that follows a whisper and, in an instant, leave us disheveled and concussed to the degree that we are left without a single word or more to speak.

Poetry can be found universally ... not only upon the stars but between them as well. It might be seen in the hearts of the kind and caring or in the eyes of the disillusioned. It could be observed in the dust particles that float in directionless slow motion in the air of a room lit only by slatted sun streaks through the blinds of a window. It might be heard in the hearty laughter of old black men as they sit and tell tales on a dilapidated porch of a shotgun house in the Mississippi Delta summer. It is the scent of sawdust after a rain or of pine that that is brought to us by an infrequent, but welcomed, New Augusta breeze.

Poetry may give as much courtesy to the mystery of God as it might to the removal of a scab; or it might elevate the scab to be above religious fare and not give a thought to any possible consequence.

Poetry is not to be owned or governed by men in the dusk of their lives who claim to have studied all of the relevant poets from the beginning of time and sit upon a lofty perch espousing style, meter, pentameter, form, right, wrong, good and bad ... at universities where God may visit but cannot stay.

Poetry is not to be escorted, guided, advised, corrected, lectured or disciplined. Poetry knows the meaning of all words and has felt all emotions known to man ... it cannot be deceived.

Poetry is what you want it to be to you. It cannot be what you want it to be to others.

If I were to die tomorrow having not written these words then I will have fallen short in supporting the very foundation upon which my words are written. I mean to say that poetry is many things to many people and on extremely rare occasions, if any at all, it is the same to any two people.

I cannot tell you what the writing and/or reading of poetry means to anyone other than me. I cannot provide reasons, causes, motivations or purposes of the writings of others. As succinctly as I can put it ... poetry belongs to all of us.

T. R. Ruffin

Path of Life

For some reason that I do not understand I have always viewed life in linear form. That is to say that we depart from an origin and we travel toward a destination. Although it is usually our intention to go from that original point to a stopping point as directly as possible it rarely works out that the path from anywhere to anywhere else resembles a straight line.

The terrain of life is much like the landscape of our planet. There are oceans and rivers; mountains and valleys; jungles and deserts; plateaus and caverns ... and all of these features present their own unique dangers and can alter our Path of Life.

Most people do not welcome the detours, the obstacles and the challenges that are surely to be encountered as we go from innocence to wisdom, from young to old, from birth to death. They seek to make their Path of Life as smooth and without turbulence as they possibly can. I do not criticize the many good people that live with such a mindset ... I just do not subscribe to it.

If I were to have an articulable philosophical model for traversing the Path of Life it would be – find the right speed for you, don't go recklessly so as to endanger others yet don't go forth overcautiously causing you to minimize your experience. Take detours only as a last resort. Approach all sharp curves, sudden turns, obstacles and hazards as a challenge, do not disregard your peripheral vision for you will see both good and evil in it. Assist others who have lost their way or broken down in their travels. Don't forget to stop periodically to appreciate the amazing people and things that are there along the way ... and do this now ... do not wait until you are five miles down a six mile road.

T. R. Ruffin

" … just when the caterpillar thought the world was over … it became a butterfly"

Edward Teller

A Spider Screams

in a hollowed log
along a trail no more
upon a damp and darkened floor
where no creature can see
… the hideousness

if spiders could scream
they'd scream out in ecstasy
as they suffocate their prey
and then above
in the glow
in the flow
in the throat of a sparrow
a wormy worm causes asphyxiation
and spewed blood upon feathers
floats earthward
… to the dirt
… from where it came

death upon a limb
death upon the will of nature
death upon an innocent sparrow
and regurgitated worm parts
are returned to the dirt
where insects feast upon them
and in a hollowed log
along a trail no more
… a spider screams

Rains Come

rains come and wash the streets
the dirty diseased streets
where cock sucking whores piss and puke
and spit out a good days work
a cleansing of sickness
rains come and flush the waste of man
down the gutter … into the sewer
sunlight comes
and sends the dogs of depravity scurrying
for dark holes to hide in
from where they watch the weak and timid
with steely eyes and furious breath
waiting for the return of night
to pound and madly eviscerate
rains come and remove the filth
from the conscience of man
so that he may keep his mind
and to avoid the slicing of his throat
by his very own hand
winds come and blow away
the disguise of good
exposing the preacher man
and his congregation of repentant sluts
rains come and wash away the evil
the evil that exists in the hearts of men
rains come and we feel absolved
rains come and we are greater men

Fountain of Tongues

I go back
back to my collection of smiles upon a mantel
in a glass enclosed case
I have the key
so … at my desire I can open it
and retrieve a smile … even though a contrived one
and attach it to my hideous face
and with that smile I will surely need a tongue
and there are many tongues
out there
no … over there
just beyond the Garden of Good
to the left of the House of Happy
there
… in the Fountain of Tongues
they're jumping all about
hard to grab one and hold on to it
slickery, slurpin' spittle spittin'
there are so many
and they seem to become excited as I approach
I never stay too long
just grab one and go
I finally get it in my mouth hole
and it begins to settle
takes a while for it to attach
soon enough, though
it will do as a good tongue would do
slurping up life as if death were moments away
kissy, kissy … Fountain of Tongues
kissy, kissy … flowing salivation
I'll allow them to bathe me
for cleansing is essential, my girl
I peer over the edge into the Fountain of Tongues
and get my face licked all over

She Calls Me Precious

she calls me Precious and she is my salvation
she goes with me to all great lands
and when I fear
her certain demeanor
keeps The Evil at bay

and all along the way
I'm reminded of birth
when all things were beginning
and life remained yet pure
when all of us were truly Innocent Ones

on cloudy days we walk outside
and remember life before love
it is almost not possible to recall those times
graciously so

she calls me Precious and she is my genesis
she is my Sister Spirit
she calms my furious propensities
and soothes my anguished character

on rainy days we scoff at the gods
for we have survived
no amount of blustery winds
can blow our dreams away

she follows and allows me to lead her
sweet inspiration by such tranquil lips
I am at peace with her
she resides within my heart
she calls me Precious and she is my universe

Where They Buried Our Mother

take my hand … young brother
and follow me
walk close enough behind me
so that you can know
that I shall always shield you

walk soon with me
beside me
with your eyes fixed and forward
so that you may see her

walk determinedly
with great purpose
and steadfast resolve
do not go away from me
even when you are filled
with suffocating grief
and the sadness consumes you
I will be beside you
I will lift you should you collapse
I will wrap you should you shiver

grasp my hands as firmly as you might
'til there be no more tremble
'til you feel ease
wipe clear your tears
and say to her what you will
for she is listening

then follow me … sweetest child
let us leave her be
let us go away
so that they may return her to the earth

follow me … walk with the strength of man
walk with me toward the vast uncertainty
where together there
we can someday soon
wake to the light of a brilliant sun

The Gods Bring Down the Rains

the gods bring down the rains
so that beneath the darkening sky of dusk
and over yet another young child
… there is a cleansing

were we all not once children?
were we all not once stainless?
… as clean as nothing

then the spirits make of us beggars
… faithless and aimless heretics

and our journeys are and will be forever …
… perilous
… though we have not yet been defeated

onto the freshly turned earth
fall the salty tears of our mothers
where there
we are left to rot
and dissolve into the ground

the grass grows upon our souls
and thus we are forgotten

so the gods bring down the rains
and wash away the sorrow
so the gods bring down the rains
and was away the pains

Words That Before I Failed to Speak

if I raised up my hands
to some perfect heaven
beyond impenetrable clouds
if I collapsed onto an unforgiving earth
and from bloodied knees
I did bellow
much as a beggar … much as a broken spirit
if I bowed my shame filled head
so it could go no lower
and submitted to all above me
if I were to offer
unto the most discerning god
my own last breath
if I were to … from now evermore
serve an insidious master
and see no more of light
if I could provide great amounts of treasure
to the merciless
if I were to do these things
and do them without delay
do them in earnest manner
could she be returned?
could she be yet once more of life?
could she be brought again to breathe?
could I see her smile at least for a moment?
could I speak to her a mere few words … could I might …
… only words that before I failed to speak?

Castrated Monks

hover about the body ... sweet angels
flutter your wings so slowly and softly
that you are barely aloft
so that the breath of God flows 'cross his skin

... and let there be a soothing
calming all disturbance
quelling any dissonance
hover sweet angels ... hover 'til there be no more tears

... let there be comfort
even as The Death takes from him his soul
and he is then no more than flesh, bone and dust
hover sweet angels ... hover 'til fear is not present

... let him hear a song
a melody of sanctuary
sung by castrated monks
such musical ecstasy
go blessed child ... go to your heaven
go away from earthly binds
the hovering angels will take you there
the castrated monks will sing you there
hear me o' young one
as I can barely speak
... and be understood
but go now and be among the unburdened
your mother will be comforted
through and through
though she will yet yearn for one more smile
... from you

sweet angels rise up this child
raise him upon mighty arms before his god
thrust him forward to the heavens
and proclaim him no more of death than alive

angels of sweetness
blow your breath forcefully into him
… cause him to spit death from his lungs
… cause him to spew forth the bile of humanity
… cause my son to breathe yet another breath
so I can look into his eyes

and whisper comfort to him
as castrated monks sing soothingly

The Once Fanciful Southern Belle

tequila bit like a dirty rattlesnake
venom spit
into a cup to be examined
the once fanciful southern belle was stoned
after all

and they thrashed about as beasts
primal and guttural
without regard for the living

gravel embedded in a dead face
all because he turned away
a badge wears a black band

Pistolero wife
nursed him back to health
then sucked him dry of vitality

back on the black highway
awakened by a dream
struck head on by the truth

parched lips parted slightly
painfully failing to make words
tongue licked to wet

she tasted the vigor
as if it were her calling
bitter and of rusted steel
excepting interruption
she bred continuously
though no seed attached
tequila stung like a maddened hornet

Old Photograph

I have an old photograph of you
and though the edges are torn
and the corners have peeled
and the color has yellowed
and for many years this old image
… has been at rest
… beneath a box
… in a dark and damp basement
… of a modest house
… in an immoral town
… that was once our home
I have an old photograph of you

I have an old photograph of you
and though I have not seen it
.. in as many years
since I've seen you
I now clutch it in hand
.. by a mighty steel grip
.. so that it may not escape me
.. forever and as long as I may breathe
because it is of you

I have an old photograph of you
.. in a pose that I do recall
.. on the hood of a car
.. in much need of repair
.. on a country lawn
.. in an apparent summer
.. in some happy time
.. in some year before me
and I cannot remove
my tired and weary eyes
from this old photograph

because it is of you

I have an old photograph of you
.. when you were a girl
.. when you were not troubled

.. when you were not encumbered
.. when you could then smile
in some time before me
.. when you were then free
.. to be just you

I have an old photograph of you
.. and though it has faded
.. and though it is fragile
.. as much as was your heart
I can still discern
.. a hint of me
.. in your smile and eyes

so this old photograph of you
I shall keep with me
until I exist no more
'til the end of my time
because it is what only remains
of what I can touch of you

\

Another Wicked Hour Moon

my son
my son of sons
rests there
there ... upon ancient hill
there ... upon the falling breath of whispers
in an earthly nest
leaves fall and cover him over
and keep him with comfort
on nights of storms
when the wind brings the spirits
I can see her
as she goes there to him
and she speaks in soft tone
my daughter
beautiful daughter of her mother
with flowing dress and sorrowful whimpers
she stands above him and begs him
bellows so
to rise ... rise ... rise
and become to life
I can see the glow of the wicked hour moon
through her dancing hair
and she kneels and finally lays above him
and with her precious hands
she sweeps the dirt that beneath he sleeps
she is his only visitor
for I cannot go there
to him
I am weakened and without courage
defeated by a death not my own
and I am filled with shame
I am no father
not worthy of yet another breath
she weeps and tears fall onto hallowed ground
and she pleads for him to rise
she is heard to ask of the gods
... for sweet mercy
yet they cannot return him here
they cannot beat again his heart

so he remains there
on such barren hill
with but one forsaken tree
and before the dawn
she will leave him be
until the storms return
and then comes
another wicked hour moon

I'll Have the Seconal After All

crazy nutfuckin' goat stranglin' spine tappin' place
in which I dwell
exist, mind you
not flourish

here come ol' Needle Bitch
swishin' and swashin'
down the Corridor of Perpetually Fluid Insanity
carryin', yep, you guessed it .. a giant ass numbin' needle
I really don't like her one bit

but who am I to register a complaint?
just another squirrel in the cage

oh despair ... ... my hair
is on nutfuckin' fire
and so they call me a hothead

I run right into the electrical maniacal fence
and it electrofried my deeply stimulated brain

I walk as a zombified cunninglingual creature
from here to there
but nowhere

they put bolts in my head
and stabilized my life
I am personally thankful
but publicly I am livid

if not mistaken
I might've truly been raped
in bacon
yes
by little piglet cockettes
in and out of my non-lubricated ears

oh the horror
and shame

imagine how silly
my testimony
before the portly judge
a Mister Boar

I've been through a lot
so, yes, my lady, my voluptuousness,
my sympathetic mind mistress, my concubine of carnality,
my princess of pharmaceutical slumber,
my master of soothing chemical arrangements
yes, oh yes ... my love

... I'll have the Seconal after all

where on god's toxic earth can a man get a witness?
just one damn witness

Pretty Good Bad Man

I have killed men that needed killing
but I have not harmed a woman or child

I have tasted the flavors that flow and glow
… through copper pipes and the natural earth
but I have not yet hit the nasty nail

I have laid with tens and hundreds
of mostly decent women
but I loved every one of them

I have taken that what I did not own
but I never took from a man what he could not spare

it would be reasonable
that when I go before judgment
to say
… that I was a pretty good bad man

I've hosted evil spirits in my head
and evicted them promptly as they got out of hand
I have been slovenly and slothful at times
but I was tidy
and unconquerable when it mattered most

Ive told tall tales and downright lied
to many good folks
but I did just so to shield their souls
… from the horrific truth

I've fathered children and forgotten their names
but I did always warn them to be unlike me
so … if it makes any difference at all
please consider me to be
a pretty good bad man

Community Guillotine

woke up sweat wet on a rainy Sunday morning
in a feverish fervor
pain was beautifully unbearable
ran down to the community guillotine
stuck my head in the head hole
just as the instructions instructed
braced myself
pushed the "Slice Your Fucking Head Smoothly Off" button

and

nothing ...
nothing happened

oops ... I'll be damned
forgot to put my quarter in the slot
pulled my head out
checked my pockets for some change a jingling
no change at all
not even a dollar bill
heard a man behind me
turned to see
he had an impatient look about him
told me that I needed to get to the end of the line
said he was in a motherlovin' hurry
to slice his fucking head smoothly off
just like everyone else in line

Boy of Beyond

of oddly appearing bugs
… he is just as curious
of warm embraces from a mother
… he is just as desirous
of all that life affords the children
… he is just as worthy
… he is of the Innocent Ones
and he knows nothing of deference
thus he will not be without steady determination
this child of God
this little man of mercy
this boy of beyond
owns my heart
by his rapid breath
he goes forward and fearless
for he is not aware of triviality
and only what matters to most
weighs heavily upon him
running and jumping and dirt and all things boy
… he is no less of them
of those that know him
… he has unto a critical humanity
given them hope beyond inspiration
his angel wings are opened
so that I may be sheltered
and there, upon the peaks of mountains
flows across the wind of the breath of God
that gave us this boy of beyond
so that we once could know of love

~~ for Rece "man" Gilder
a friend

The Suck

up on that hill there
where from it he can see
the souls gathered below his feet

he wonders
just how many
of those lost
he can lift
from the muck
of the suck
the suck of the earth
the suck of man

he can pull them
with mighty effort
from there
where vigor is forcefully sucked
from all good men

he can reach down
and they will grasp him
and the suck shall be
violently released

he can do this …
… unsuck
the suck

Black Church

cold air
stung his face
on his way
to the Black Church

boy walked a country mile
to get where he thought he belonged

boy heard the sangin' and the carryin' on
heard them laughing ... heard them happy
such a beautiful sound
comin' through the cracks of that ol' Black Church

every Sunday mornin' ... then again that evenin'
found him walkin' by
the Black Church

boy could smell some cookin'
in the crisp country air
mixed with the scent of pine
some kinda hog
some kinda greens
sho' smelled good
to this unfed boy
up in the Black Church
so he just kept on walkin' by
again and again
so he could hear 'em sangin'
and hollerin'
'bout that fella ... Jesus
up and again down the hill
in the middle of the gravel road
kickin' rocks like he didn't give a care
but he did ...

onliest reason he was there
was 'cause of the Black Church

boy never did tell nobody
'bout going down there
to the Black Church
weren't nobody to tell
Granny was old
and mama was gone
on business
was what he was told

boy lived all week fer the mornin' of Sundays
didn't have to be woked up
didn't have to be gettin' yelled at
to get up and go
on his way
to the old Black Church
he just went
on his very own

didn't matter none 'bout no rain
didn't matter none 'bout no cold
didn't matter at all 'bout no sweatin'
long as he got to get to walk by
the Black Church

sometimes they sang the same songs
other times they'd try a new one or two
sooner than he knew, though,
he could sang every word with 'em
and sang he did

on a summer Sunday mornin'
inside the Black Church
in the middle of a song
the Reverend James raised his hands
and lowered them
hushing them quiet
and bent a curious ear t'ward the outside
as they settled

they all heard it
they heard what they could not believe
they could hear someone sangin'

out there on the road
the voice of an angel
a voice like they'd never before heard
surely the voice of God in Heaven

the door slowly opened
and the Black Church emptied
they saw him
he was there
just 'cross the yard
out in the road
walkin' and kickin' rocks
and sangin'
sho' nuff sangin'

the dirty faced white boy
hadn't yet seen 'em
so he kept right on sangin'

the Black Church black folk were stunned
by what they heard
tears filled their eyes

they'd seen the boy before
some of the sisters worried 'bout him
but they was told better not to meddle
so they just prayed for him
but now …
here he was
sangin' their song
word for every blessed word
in a voice that was as sweet and pure
as the whisper of Jesus

boy finished the song
and as if he felt their presence
he turned to them
as saw them looking at him
and he became frightened
like he done did somethin' wrong

so he started to run
Reverend James bellowed in a hearty voice
"stop there, boy ... do not run!"

and he stopped

Reverend James spoke to him

"boy, please come inside ... you are welcome here"

the boy was not sure he ought to go in there
up in the Black Church
he had not been told not to
but he didn't know 'bout them black folk
he'd been told by his grandfather
that white folks ought stay away from black folks
it was just how it should be

so he said to Reverend James,

"but I'm white"

the Reverend James walked to the boy
slow as not to cause him fear
the Reverend reached to the boy and took his hand
and as he led the boy to the Black Church ... he said,

"yes, that you are ... you are white ... and yes, we are black ...
we are different ... but we are the same ... but inside of this
church we are all of but a single color ... "

the boy interrupted,

"what color is that?"

"well son ... it is an indescribable color ... you cannot see it but you can feel it ... it is warm and it is comforting ... this color that we are is the most magnificent color on earth ... it is radiant and it is of peace ... the color we are is soothing of the soul ... it pleases all who feel it ... it is healing ... it is bright when you need light ... it is dim when you need rest ... this color is for everyone ... it does not hurt you ... it does not distress you ... it does not judge you ... contrarily it wraps you in tranquility and gives you great ease ...... son, we are the color of love"

and with that
the dirty faced white boy walked into the Black Church
and he was accepted
with wide open arms
he was loved
for he had not been before
he was fed
he was cleansed
he was happy in his heart
and on every Sunday thereafter
he walked that country mile
wearing a great big smile
and he sang among them
because he was one with them
and one of them

... in the Black Church

Who Will Be My Keeper This Day?

who will be my captor
upon the young morning
when the sun sneaks through
in thin slivers
and I am caught
always mesmerized by the particles of dust
floating
with no aim or direction
in and among and out the sunbeams
attempts to count them
or name them
or follow any particular one
to see where it might go
results ... without fail ... in mind numbing frustration

who will be my keeper today?
will she be
from the university?
will she be friendly enough
to speak to me?
could it be a youthful boy
not from here
but from anywhere else
being indoctrinated
to hate
the likes of me?
would he be
of the mind
to offer to me
a parcel of sweet candy
or to slice my throat?
might it be
an old man
who has it in his head
that I am a serpent
enemy to man
or may the old man
hold slight sympathy
for a man like me?

who will be my enslaver this day
when all of man is unencumbered?
or will it be only me

that leaves me to be

not free?

Hypnotizing Thrust Monkey

I keep dreaming of her
even upon waking
I keep seeing her
even upon closing my eyes
I keep hearing her voice
even upon covering my ears
I keep tasting her
even upon cutting my tongue from my mouthhole
I keep thinking of her
even though I boiled my brains
… to keep from doing so

she done put it on me
put it on me good
she done put that hypnotizing thrust monkey
on me
all up on me
and I can't shake it
can't shake it off me
it's all over me
I need an exterminator
I need a trapper
I need an exorcist
something or somebody
come get this godforsaken hypnotizing thrust monkey
and kill it

To Remain Not Mentioned

it is peculiar
that
when I lived
they passed me by
and did not hazard one glance
in my direction
they took no notice
of what slight good I was
and they did not part their lips
to speak of me
they did not recognize me
I was a subject
to remain
not mentioned

and they did not practice
the religion they played

but when I walked with The Death
toward the end
they returned to me
being guided by guilt
and gathered by the force of obligation
The Death would permit me to see
on occasion
the faces of my creation
and of my own dear mother and father
and I saw upon them
contempt
and an inner contempt
forced brows to raise
and mouths to be affixed ... downward

I heard them say
in quiet company and confidence
things that I should not have
and I heard them speak of retribution
and that this was now my own

paradoxically

when *The Death* took me from them
and the others
and all that I've known
and I was incinerated
and bone was but dust

then
they spoke of me in contradicting tone
I was a man of vision … of honor … of courage
such a good man
I was good … good … goody fucking good

and the tears flowed down pampered cheeks
on demand
cutting eyes to see if any one bought it
words …
more kind than they thought I deserved …
were spoken
by a man of the cloth
and he spoke as if he knew me
but he did not

and then I was no more
but with the wind
when I was gone … gone … long fucking gone
they traveled separate paths
to their own imperfect homes

and they had not practiced
the religion they played

and I am forever
… to remain not mentioned

Mess My Mind

she's known to come skippin' down the road at odd enough times
with a basket full of happy
clickin' and clackin'
clappin' and slappin'
givin' and gettin'
and sho' messin' my mind
bless her kuntry heart ... bless her simple ways
I give her kisses for she loves them so
I really like the way
she's drunk before noon
and naked not long after
sho' messin' my mind
she's known to lose her direction from here to there
but always finds her way back home
usually by Monday
she brings me great gifts of things she made
damn if I were to know what they are
but because these things are of her hand
I will cherish them for my life
she's known to jump and shout without warning
at something she thinks be funny
scares the bejesus out of me
makes me some kinda nervous
but that's why I love her
bless her mama and no 'count daddy
for if not fer them
she wouldn't be who she is
and I wouldn't have her 'round
sho' messin' my mind
she's known to scratch me 'cross my back
just 'cause she can
she can be a handful or more
but when I am able to hold her
there's nothin' better in the world
she really messes my mind
she has me all twisted and some kinda crazy
when she's gone I miss her
but when she's home I'm with her
she's known to drive an old truck
carryin' a load of pulpwood

and cussin' like she had a reason
she's all the time bein' tough
but she aint nothin' but a girl
she don't let nobody close
'cept me
I really like the way she sings in a whisper
softly
into my ear
and she says things
that sho' mess my mind

Drunker Than a Sugar Mill Jackass

was in a bar
in Jackson, Mississippi
was drunker than a football bat
and I damn well knew it
met a girl
from Pelahatchie
she was drunker than a bicycle
and she damn well knew it
if I were to be asked
how she looked
I'd have said
she had a great personality

"last call" shouted out the bartender man
he was drunker than Cooter Brown
so we ordered another round
and one for the road

girly girl drove us in her Buick
she was drinkin' and a drivin'
I was drinkin' and a ridin'
we were drunker than two blind coons
on a merry-go-round

I asked her, I said, "where we goin', Sistah Spirit?"
said she was takin' me home ... with her
"we goin' to Pela-by-damn-hatchie?" I screamed
like a school girl gettin' tickled
she just smiled ... an electric smile
and drove on through the black night
she was drunker than a pickled egg
I tried to diddle with her
'cause I was drunker than a two-headed catfish

next thing remembered was a voice in my head
louder and louder became this voice
I opened my eyes and to my surprise
a face was starin' right into my face
and that voice that I heard in my head
was comin' from this face real close to my face

the voice of the face was sayin' somethin'
somethin' like, "get yo ass outta that car, boy!!"
I was drunker than a monkey on a unicycle

I removed myself from Hoochie Mama's hoopdie ride
and the first thing I noticed
was that the big black Alabama State Trooper did not appear to be
in a good mood
he was sober
and I was drunker than ten screamin' lesbians what done fell in a
fountain of tongues

… later that day
after the mother of the Princess of Pelahatchie had bailed us out
I found myself sittin' right there in a pick-up truck between the
Queen of Pelahatchie and her sad-eyed, lip-poked-out, hung-the-
hell-over, drink-any-man-under-the-table, cuss-like-a-sailor,
flash-her-teats-at-the-drop-of-a-hat, deer-huntin', perch-jerkin',
good-time-havin'-daughter

and we were on the way back

the uncomfortable silence was deafening
so I decided to ask …. to no one in particular

I said, "what, in the name of Schlitz Malt Liquor, happened back
there? How did we wind up in Ala-fuckin'-bama?"

well, I should not have broken the silence
'cause once I did it put my future wife's mama into orbit
and she lit into her daughter like there weren't gonna be no
tomorrow.
then it got bad and Sugar Tits cussed her mama somethin' fierce

I'm sure glad we were dang near the exit to Pelahatchie
when she slid that ol' truck to a screachin' stop
right there in the middle of I-20
… causing folks that was behind us to go to screachin' and slidin'
and cussin' and drivin' all up into the pine trees.

she put us out and didn't even look once in her rear view mirror

me and my true love of not yet 24 hours started to walkin'
we had nothin' but the clothes we was wearin'
oh, and a toothbrush from the Birmingham city jail
just to get a rise out of her I asked her … with a serious face …
I said, "well, do you think your mother likes me?"
She looked at me kinda odd like … with her head sort of canted
just so … she had that crazier-than-a-pit-bull-on-meth look in her
eyes

all of a sudden it was on
me and my prize of a woman engaged in a knock-down-drag-out,
mother of all domestic scraps right there 'side the road, near
Pelahatchie, Mississippi

damn country coon dog woman bloodied my lip and I passed out at
the sight of my own blood

when I came to … devilwoman was gone.
I stuck out my thumb and hitched a ride
back to Jackson
right back to where I started
at the same damn bar I was at the night before
where
not too long after I sat down
I met a girl
from Puckett

she was drunker than a sugar mill jackass

The Tossing of Things Inanimate

she liked to throw things
crash 'em up against the wall
anything and everything
any item at all
nothing was sacred
even the bible of Gideon was not spared
the telephone … alarm clock … lamp … whatever

and this enthusiasm was encouraged
… though not enthusiastically
for then … if so
she might have moved buildings
of magnificent structure
and that I could not have afforded
and good God of Grapes … I was ever so responsible

I woke with a face glazed with emotion
it has since been cleansed
I think

Fifty-Two Year Drive

me and sister been gone
gone a long time
we been livin'
some kinda livin'
been on the sicker than anything road of suck
but me and sister
we been through it
and come out smellin'
smellin' quite foul

been gone a mighty long time
haven't heard mama's voice in 52 years
can't remember for the war
can't see for the tears
can't keep on goin' like we was
me and sister been rollin'
and preachin'
and kissin' babies
and dreamin' 'bout
the coming of the lawd

we been down to the next town
just drivin' 'round
and lookin'
lookin' for mama
nobody had done seen mama
didn't know nothin' about her
well, I'll just be fucked without so much as a kiss

where'd ya go my only mama?
me and sister been lookin' a long time for ya
they told us to check out Corpus or Brownsville even
may even have gone on up to Galveston
if she did I sho she could've already been gone
on up to the Lawd in the heavens
sho nuff hopes she happy
I think she would have a nice smile
if it were that I could ever see it

me and sister
done been on a ride
we been listening to Jesse Mae
she be sangin'
like I be feelin'
good

me and little sister
been on a 52 year drive

just a peepin'
and keepin' our red eyes peeled
for our precious mama

The Precious Indignity

out of the womb
into the room
a birthing alone
is not love

sugarplums in the putrid slums
put another infantile log on the fire
warm this room with the flesh of the innocent ones
because, god damnit, those of us still living are freezing

put them in the garbage of the day
send them merrily on their way
raise 'em up to be nobody's fool
kick 'em ... slap 'em ... send 'em to school

life is given
then removed

it is brittle
it is frail
it is cruel
it is horrid

... thankfully
it is brief

sweet boy never had a chance
spent his eighth birthday
in a shelter with mom
ceremonious banter was not had
someone sang to him
someone gave him a cookie
that's all they could

later ... as if it were written ... boy went east
and there ... there upon unbearable nights
the screams and bellows
eventually faded
by the faithful method
of self-soothing chemicals

sweetest boy became a man
and it would seem
on his way
toward, again, a great uncertainty

he died vacantly
on a Monday morning

and there were a few others
at the throat of one another
duplicitous fucks that lied to him daily
and we expected more?

go rest your weary head
son of someone
child of the rut
go be with a comforting god

surely there is one
and among the indifferent
emerges a sister
she shall carry on
his cause for cleansing
his yearning for acceptance
she shall make righteous
the precious indignity

~~ with Jana Barlow Feldman
in loving memory of Phillip Barlow 1978-2009

What the Girlie Girls Feed Him

eclectically driven by a madness not yet identified
ain't no fucking nature here, boy
it's all about the gloomy steel city
and the barren chambers of his heart

upon what does this man among boys feast?
one would suppose he devours
... what the girlie girls feed him

where does this human beast lay his head?
one might imagine
in the lap of accommodating whores

behavioral progress was observed and noted
but that was the distant past
his pornographic memory sparked a relapse
and there were everlasting psychocosmic visions
big boy screwed his sister
then cut his nuts out with a twisted root beer can
dichotomy of pleasure and pain
maladaptive son of an opiate afternoon

history predicts a path
that mighty man just may follow
the probability is great
resistance is low
ain't no fucking emotion here, boy

it's all about wiping tears from a terrifically stoic face
environmental occurrences are the determining factors
this boy never had a chance
in pursuit of the absolute climactic event
there is no end to the means
mortal sensation is paramount
ain't no fucking rules here, boy

Wisdom Window

from the view of a blurred and unaffected Wisdom Window
I see

I see .... things

what is brought before me
across the vastness
nothing less than
the expansive transvisional sound of a gutting

on a slab
of frozen concrete
lay my innards
and steam rises slowly from them
in no discernable hurry
dissipating and becoming transparent
of less substance
mimicking life
before my birth
I could feel

upon bare breasts
I rest a weary head
for just before
I sit
at the Wisdom Window
I emerge
and with delicate thought
I resist

all that I see
from the view
of the Wisdom Window

I fear

Take Me Home

in the fields
on the rows
searing sun
blistered skin
black man keeps moving
lest he be beaten
beyond his sensibilities

... so he sings ... he bellows
from untamed throat

       take me home ... take me home, Jesus
       take me home to where I belong

seeds blow
by wicked winds
to distant fertile earth
and grow
man keeps moving
lest he be lashed
to bloody shreds

... so he sings ... he moans
in rhythmic sorrow

       take me home ... take me home, Jesus
       take me home to where I belong

tears well
but are not released
through watered eyes
he can see the truth
man keeps moving
lest he become no more to be a man
and then they will have defeated him

... so he sings ... he cries
in desperate finality
       take me home ... take me home, Jesus
       take me home to where I belong

Gift Giver

beneath threatening skies
along dangerous avenues
and among a wicked humanity
she arrived there
where I would soon be

there she waited
… and waited
… and waited
as patiently and as dignified
as any young person could be

sitting
back straightened in perfect form
a little lady
silently and humbly waiting

and when I did approach
and saw her there
a smile appeared
and things were well
to be at face level
I bent to a knee
to be able to see
whatsoever she concealed
beyond her electric eyes

and I asked her in calm tone

"from what distant pathway have you traveled?
and at what great peril have you come to visit me?
what evil have you encountered
on your journey
… to my heart?

how many stars have you counted
as you made your way through darkness?
and did you somehow know that I would
… one day
be waiting beneath those very stars

... for you?
who might have harmed you?
and by the mercy of what god
shall I spare his life?"

and though she was taken aback
she faltered none
and held out her hands in presentation
a gift of one
a gift by her gracious hand
and of her golden heart
so I accepted her offering
no words were spoken
I was not able

I returned her
in safe measure
to her home
where I last saw her
as she turned to wave

then in an instant
she was there no more
but she will stay with me always
in my hardened heart
my little traveler
my little gift giver

Johnny Insignificant

" ... pray for war ... pray for war
I can't hear you ... say it !!
... pray for war ... pray for war
louder !! .. say it with me
...pray for war ... pray for war"

unidentified Drill Sergeant
Fort McCellan, AL
1983

little sister asked again
to anyone that might be listening
 "when my brother gonna be home?"
big sister said again
"I don't know, Lil' Bit ... I just don't know"
and a teardrop fell ...
slow motion
seemingly hours before it exploded onto the floor
and was heard
as ground-shaking and as loud
as any bomb the War Pigs could make

mother couldn't stand erect long enough to see anyone
enough sedation for the nation
daddy was out in the shop
wouldn't let nobody in
been in there for hours
ever since the sheriff and the chaplain came by
sheriff said to leave him be

girlfriend was in her dorm room
hundred or so miles away
collapsed in her mother's lap
who came to school
to deliver the news
before she heard it elsewhere

he volunteered
and they trained him
then sent him to fight

there was a cause ... some point ... somewhere
but he didn't know it
didn't know the reason for it
didn't really matter to him
followed orders
that's what he did
and did so honorably
and courageously
and with valor
and without question
... for his country

and he went there
wherever
with *The Death* nipping at his heels
relentlessly

and when it was all over
he came home
to hugs and celebrations
he was a hero
and he was revered by all
and a bleached blonde reporter interviewed him
live ...
from beside a truck with a satellite dish
way up high in the happy sky
but the crowd went home
and Johnny Anybody
found himself alone
and before long
he had sweat the bed wet
and was sick
and infected
and damaged
and deranged
not himself anymore

so Johnny Nobody looked to the War Pigs for help
and the suit clad swine squealed in incredulous tones
that there was nothing they could do for him
that their hands were tied
no monies appropriated

no medicines
no biggie
it will subside
good luck
goodbye

so he just dealt with it
as long as he could
until he could not
weren't so easy for him
to take the easy way out
several attempts were made
the last being a grand success
Johnny Nobody done gone and did it
yes he did
done gone and blowed his brains
all over the bathroom

somebody had to bury good ol' Johnny Anybody
who done went over there
… to where god pukes and shits and
and got himself all messed up

big sister took care of it all
mom just stared at the ground
dad wore sunglasses … would not remove them

and the bleached blonde reporter reported
live …
from beside a truck with a satellite dish
way up high in the sad day's sky
outside of the jam packed church
she said good things about ol' Johnny Insignificant
of course
and then she said, "back to you, Bob"
with an incongruent smile

Bob did his best to deliver the obligatory sad face
while shaking his head and speaking words of sincerity
he failed …

… commercial break

There Be No Nights

there be no nights
like the one before this day's night
and the ones before last night
and the million many more before …
… for that is when I dreamed of her

there be no nights
like this day's night
and tomorrow's night
and the million many more that shall follow …
… for that is when I will hold her

and there will be no nights
of any known nights
of all God's nights
that were before or followed …
… that I will allow harm ever to her

Cold, Cold Floor

if you find me at all
if you happen to search your sinister mind
… where you usually keep me
I might not be there
I might have gone away
… from your twisted vision

if you even effort
if you should have any concern
if you are not completely consumed
… by an apathetic toxicity

you will then find me here
simply at my end
 beneath the feet of man

on the cold, cold floor

Country Joe Jesus

it's all about thrillin' and chasin'
all about getting' next to the next one
it's all about Percy havin' mercy
and Country Joe Jesus
it has to do with blasphemy
and government sanctioned pornography
it must be because of My Lai
that we be drinkin' Mai Tais
Cadillac the Corner Boy said the word
and skulls went to crackin'
Billy Boy from Hot Springs
needed some backin'
so the whores on Green Street
kept on shootin' straight up in the main vein
never knew if Mookie was a spooky
but he woke up dead in the Ironbound
in a trash filled alley
next to the finest Portuguese restaurant
in all of Newark
cold and hungry vacant eyed babies
just inside of sooty brick walls
just outside of view
so we drove right on by
and however high the ladder would reach
we would climb it
and jump right down in it
into the pile of vile humanity
punk bitch Italian made men
were no match for the rat walkers
of Washington Heights
glory be to the god of decadence
half lesbian Latino cuties and Cuban translators
kept us occupied at night
when the dreams came
they were good enough to hold us
'til the shakin' went away
and on some cloudy, smoggy day
Barry went and got shot
by the hand of his own man
and the bagpipes ring loudly in our ears

Closer to Home

if there were to be
any way
on any day
o' pleasant stranger
for you to lift me
and direct me
or even take me
... a little closer to my home
I would give you
all that I have
all that I own

I am the burden ... now
I am reliant
upon the graciousness
of the hand
of the lot of humanity
but
regrettably
not of the one I love

The Persistent Return of Michi Pfau

I did not dress like a damn government man
but I was one

and when I was over there
no one knew it
for the longest time
and that was how it had to be ... to save me

I usually slept by day
and roamed the streets
of the gloomy steel city at night
and I'd taken to sleeping wherever
and eating whatever the girlie girls would feed me
that's how it had to be
in the name of God, country
and the perpetual pursuit of the wicked

so at the dusk of the day
I'd kiss her on her cheek
and slap her on her ass
and off I'd go .. out the door
and into the black night
and, of course, toward great uncertainty

my job was that of a liar
deceit was my craft
but it soon became my reality
I straddled the proverbial fence
so I could see over
into a land of all that was evil

and on occasion I would cross over into The Empty
and see just how far I could go
and then to return just in time

no one knew the real me
and neither did I
'til the fateful night I met my Michi Pfau
and from then ever forward
I have known the real me

and that is because
my Michi Pfau has not left me

just because she is no longer of this earth
and because it is by my hand
just because she breathes no more
and I am the reason

just because I am the one who failed her
Michi Pfau returns to me

she is ever more as beautiful as before
even now as an apparition

she comes to me in my dreams
and thus … I beg of sleep to come … rapidly
to bring her to me
she sits cross legged at my side
and looks at me in whimsical fashion
and she uses silence … more silence … even more
and as the guilty are prone to do
they cannot tolerate such silence
so they disrupt it with lies

and my Michi Pfau will appear
at any uncertain time
and she will cast her rhetorical gaze upon me
and say nothing

I find myself stuttering and stammering
and wholly uncomfortable
until she's heard enough
of my apologies and penitence

then she slightly but warmly smiles
and I am at ease
for the moment

as suddenly as she appeared … she is vanished
and I find myself empty
I live with constant eagerness
awaiting her return

though because of her
I now know
who I really was

I was a liar with cause
I was the master of deception
I was a multifarious character
I was who I needed to be
I was a government mule

I know this now
for the persistent return of Michi Pfau

Message to Mother

you can rest now
… my troubled mother
you can finally rest

you can be without disturbing dissonance
you can be with ease
you can exhale your conflicted life
and spit societal bile at your feet

I have found him
yes, I have found him
… my sorrowful mother
I have found him
and he is well

he has loved
and he has been loved
he holds no contempt
he has only a curiousness
and I shall bring him
to where he can know you

I told him
yes, I told him
my suffered mother
that you searched for him
that you longed for him
that you loved him

you should know
that when he smiles
it is you that smiles
and when I look into his eyes
I see you there

you can rest now

Death in Cotton

over the endless expanse
of the barren fields
a fog of apathy hovered still and quiet
not unlike a thousand nights before
it would remain

but on that night
on that night when
the air was thick
with a lending of barbarian temper

his legs in full stride
cut sharply the undisturbed mist
boy kept running
not toward
but from something
… something wicked
… something vile
from The Evil

of The Evil
boy was familiar
but he had not yet encountered
such wickedness
though when it did come to him
it would not relent
boy did flee

throughout the blackest of nights
he ran as a ghost
as fast as he could
for minutes and hours
for not but a mile but twenty

and as he could not tire
and he could not stop
boy heard them
he heard them speak
he heard them breathe
whispers grew to screams

as he had no other means
… no god of mercy
… no defender of humanity
he could not be but commanded
by their emphatic direction

boy turned sharply
and reversed his path
and as horrid as it was
on his escape into the great void
his return unto the judgment of man
was even more … if imaginable
sinister

the Hounds of Dark Hell
nipped and spit and growled
from angry throat
at the heels of this boy
in relentless pursuit
pushed boy onward
onward toward uncertainty

when boy arrived
unto civil man's view
his presence was not announced
he had followed the urgings
of those unknown
and now his fate
belonged to those with veiled face
and eyes of deception

boy stood at the foot of a marker
constructed as stone
erected exactly center
of a fair village

who, now, would allow harm
to such a boy?
not the town's people
surely not his own

but as the sun rose distant
appearing above ancient trees
a sound was heard
from the marker of truth

and a slight piece fell
onto the earth
and awkwardly rolled and tumbled
coming to a rest
at the feet of young boy

as it would be
though should not have been
the statue of justice
and humane action
crumbled at first slow ... then rapid

and in immeasurable time
boy stood among the fine dust
which once before
represented human compassion

upon the next night fall
the apathetic haze
returned once more
and there could be seen
no sign of the horror
blood, bone or flesh
and certainly no sign
of victory of man

~~ with Myrna Colley-Lee

Walking the Path of Calm

oh, reverent mother
I am your reprobate son
... feed me for I am starving
... bathe me for I am covered by a glaze of carnal filth
... harbor my fugitive inclinations
... burn me at the stake
... incinerate my unsalvageable soul
so that I may walk the Path of Calm

oh, reverent mother
I have lived there
... in swine bowels
... among the callous hearted creatures of religion
... among mankind
... beneath the cloven hooves of humanity
... upon the wings of vulture clergymen

oh, reverent mother
hold my fragile hand and walk me
... walk me down the Path of Calm
... feed my palpable hunger
... quench my insatiable desire for fleshly pleasures
... provide me with direction

come now
come now, mother
I require your guidance
before I go sideways
I must be led
come now, mother
seize my solid soul and take me there
walk me down the Path of Calm

Nonsensical Rain Dance

my injun princess could shake it
she sho' could

… she would cause me great anxiousness
… make me sweat big salty sweat
… make me dance foolishly a nonsensical rain dance
… so it might rain and douse my loins afire

made the reservation chilrens giggle at me
made the elders frown and shake their head side to side
made a lot of folks do a lot of things
but it made me love her more than one man should

if he said it once he'd said it a hundred times
my daddy would say …
"boy, don't ya go and marry no damn injun girl"
sounded like sound advice to me

so I didn't marry her
even though she birthed my three chilrens
well, not sure about one of 'em
but I know the other two are mine
cause they even do that silly raindance
just like I used to do it
it's so cute to watch 'em dance around herky jerkily
all the while slapping at their crotch with both hands

God knows … I love them half-injun rascals
they'll be fine warriors someday

from time to time my daddy asks me
if I'm still seeing that negro girl
… or that Costa Rican girl
… or that Argentiner girl
… or whatever kinda girl his senile mind can think of
and I will say …
"Pop, she aint none of that … she's injun by damnit"

and he will say …
"what kinda injun?"

and I will say …
"hell, I dunno, Seminole, Apache … somethin'"
and he will say …
"better watch them damn Apaches … they'll scalp yo ass"

and it goes on and on like that with dear ol' dad

all is good though
my injun princess still shakes it for me
and sometimes
… when the moon is full
… and the coyotes howl
… and the chilrens are sleeping in their own teepee
we might hit the peace pipe and I can be seen
by only the moonlight
dancing my nonsensical rain dance

Big Ass Sexy Mama

big mama … big sexy
I have a thing for you
big mama … big ass sexy
big o' mama

I have a thing for you
   it's only love

I woke up way too early this afternoon
and big mama … you was sho' nuff on my mind

big mama you cook collard greens
like there aint gonna be no damn tomorrow

with a hog jowl simmerin'
and slow bubblin' in a big ass pot
enough grease to stop an elephant heart

what ya gonna do without me Big Mama?
Cause I'm going on a little trip
all the way to Alamagordo … as in New Mexico

I hope ya miss me
I hope ya miss me bad
'cause I know I'm gonna miss my big ass sexy mama

but when I come home you could be waitin' on me
you could be waitin' on me wearin' nothin' but an apron

oh my … oh my big mama
my big sexy
my princess of big ass lovin'

oh big mama you have me dreamin'
you have me dreamin' bout yo bacon drippings
and cornbread puddin'

can I get a witness? can I get a damn witness
… just one time?

you make me howl big mama
... you make me curse the days I'm not with you
you make me hungry ... but you never starve me
you make me wanna slap my own mama
oh yes you do
... yes you do my big ol' sexy ass big mama thing you

Dress and Chains

what he done gone and done?
what did he do?
what bad thing has Big Boy done done?

Big Boy with black head and eyes full of life
done gone and did it didn't he?
sun be slut sweatin' hot
scorching his already burned skin
passersby just pass on by
cuttin' eyes and whispering as whisperers do

boy sits all day on a stump
staring forward … on past the pain
into the night … 'til his head hang over
and his tongue drips blood
onto his bare, filthy feet

Big Boy slumbers now with God
'cause no earthly person would take his cause

what Big Brother done done
to be in dress and chains?

I Shall Cause the Wind to Brush Gently Your Face

if *The Death* were to come for me
on the morning of tomorrow
then I shall take with me
all of your pain and sorrow

if I could not once more
bring my lips to yours
to kiss away your troubles
and I shall bring the rains
to cleanse your soul of sadness

if I could not ever again
touch your smoothest skin
I would then send the clouds
to wrap you in warm comfort

if I could no longer have you
lay upon me
and feel your heart beat rhythmically
then I will give you guardian wolves
so that you may slumber in peace

and if it were to be true
that I must go without you
then I would go with such sadness
but if then you should think of me
and if your heart did yearn
and if you were to wonder
if you were of my thoughts
then I shall cause the wind to brush gently your face
… and you will know

Old Dog

old dog
you aint got no shame
that's just why
you aint got no name
you old dog

you aint no Old Yeller
that's for sure
you just a damned old dog
a biscuit-eatin' ... your-own-butt lickin'
old dog

flea scratchin' ... all-the-damn-time barkin'
dirty dog
you need a bath
you table-scrap eatin' ... bad breath havin'
backyard hole diggin'
old no-name dog

you aint no good fer nothin'

you big ol floppy eared ... no account
tail-barely waggin' ... layin' around
sad faced, droopy-eyed ... gettin' in my way
old dumb dog

but don't ever leave me
old dog
I aint got no body but you
old dog

Who, But John Lee?

John Lee said the homeboys sang
and boy did they ever
they sang at my birth
and again at my wedding (both of 'em)
and finally upon my death

they sang the blues
as deep and as blue as it gets
    so blue ... almost black
they weren't so much crooners
as they were the rhythm of my life

but the homeboys sang
and they sang before sunrise
and just at dusk

and the homegirls ... oh the homegirls
he loved to watch 'em swish
he kept his eyes on them
liked the way they walked
loved the way they talked
made him spellbound
made his kingsnake crawl

bye bye ... bye bye

bye bye … John Lee

bye bye ... bye bye

Grace of the Afternoon

come to me slowly merciful morning
for I have no hurry
let me see the day
for I will see no more

oh radiant sun
do not be indifferent
shine upon me intent
I am weary in the absence of light

peace could not find me
amid the deviltrolls of darkness
I shall not beg or cower
behind hell's heavy hearthstones

come to me soul salvation
bring forth goodness
do not leave me rapidly good day
for I have remaining only
but the grace of the afternoon

The Shit Poem

my son said to me
on a fine April afternoon
upon hearing a song
on the radio
playing music
as radios are prone to do

he said, "that's the shit, Dad"
I retorted
in astonished manner
"excuse me, sir!"

he spoke louder and clearer and slower
so as to be understood
as if were of feeble mind

"that song, it's the shit"

"Well, do you mean the song is shit and you don't like it?"

"no, no ... I like it indeed,
it is slang talk, Dad ... you wouldn't understand"

"the shit you say", I said
"I do understand
... and it's pretty shitty of you to say different
... I mean hell's bell's and shit fire
... I've been in the shit and it was not a good place to be
... so I don't give two shits what you say
... I fully understand
... 'cause boy, I've seen some crazy shit in my time"

"well, holy shit, Dad ... sure didn't mean to piss you off"
he said, with a shit-eatin' grin

"awe shit, son, I'm not pissed off
... I know you're just talkin' shit
... I know you got more than shit fer brains
... you're just a little shit
... but you're my little shit

… but if you get out of line
… and get to actin' crazier than a shithouse rat
… I'm gonna slap the everlovin' shit out of ya
… and it ain't gonna be for shits and giggles"
sure as shittin', he got the message

and we rode in silence
for a length of time
and upon arriving at home
his mother, my wife
met us at the door
and gave me a rash of shit
for bein' late, and muddy, and stupid
and whatever other kinda shit she could think of

so I told her,
"I've had enough of this shit"
and turned right around
got back in my truck
squealed out of my driveway
faster than greased shit
drove directly to the bar
walked in there like I was the shit
and proceeded to get shitfaced

what a shitty situation
but, alas
who gives a shit?

Old Lake

old lake
forgotten
no eyes of man lay yet upon her
she is just there
as majestic as any mind can imagine

hidden by hundred year trees
no path to
… no path fro

the sun rises lazily and late
and settles early
behind the pines
an eager darkness creeps in
old lake … a sacred place
as is a cemetery
welcoming newly freed spirits

what can you tell us, old lake?
being not yet fouled by man
might you remain pure and clear
and may we never find you
for you are worthy of solitude
you know of nothing more

Jumper

in some mid-western town
off some country gravel road
down a narrow drive of maybe six or seven miles or so
on some starless black September night
where all roads end

Baby Girl was there
she was there for no better reason
than The Empty had called her there

she climbed to the top of the fire tower
and just sat there ... just thinking
and thinking
and thinking
and thinking

things could've been different
could've been a child of the heavens
could've been pure of heart
could've been a pretty girl
but she was none of that

she listened to them
heard them say ... to one another
with condemning eyes darting to and fro
just how ass ugly she was
just how stupid ignorant she was
just how foul of body she was

so she jumped
and for the very first time
in her miserable existence
she was free ... free from the bindings of man
free of what she had learned she was
free as she floated
free ... free ... free

and when her head hit the road below
it exploded
and her beautiful mind went everywhere

the town cried for her
but the people had to blame someone, by damn
so they pointed guiltfilthy, indignant fingers
at one another

and by the hand of an angry god
it was written in words of dark clouds
in an even darker sky

" … there is shame upon you all"

People Meat

floating peacefully in a flat bottom john boat
on a Sunday afternoon
in a Mississippi June
hotter than three kinds of hell
she hadn't said a word in a good long while
just kept on casting
in no sensible direction
and it was not important
the dark water was sleepy smooth
if there were truly a heaven
we might have found it
then ... without fair warning ... or any introduction
she posed a question
and by her eyes I could tell
was of serious consequence

" ... have you ever wondered what people meat would taste like?"

I was taken aback and sufficiently alarmed
to the degree that I kept her in my sight
for the remainder of the day
I did tell her, though
with a tone of confidence
that I had not ever
in all of my years
not even once
wondered ... openly or privately
what humans may taste like
cooked or not
and at that ... she shrugged ... unaffectedly
and went about her business
casting
in no sensible direction
and it was not important

Karma Goat

Jessie Mae Hemphill was sangin'
'bout a streamline train
her black ass, cotton pickin'
country coon dog soundin' voice
was comin' out of my speakers
they was pegged out at thirty-five
on the volume thingy
that woman sho could sang
... like a molasses fed angel

windshield wipers back n' forth
somethin' stuck up in 'em
screechin' 'cross the glass
pissed me off way back when it first started rainin'
'bout ten miles south of Memphis
but I got over it
by the time we got to Robinsonville

girlie girl was knockin' back shots
of somethin' from a bottle
somethin' clear ... and straight ... and stout
and she was talkin' all out the side of her pretty head
'bout detox and rehab and rehab reunions
and crazy shit like that
she sat crosslegged ... sideways ... injun style
just a starin' at me
I heard her say ... "what ya thinkin' bout?"
I said ... "sounds good to me"
she said ... "you aint even listenin' to me"
I said ... "you damn right I aint"
she said ... "well, just why-the-hell not?"
and I said ...
"'cause you're drunker than a cross-eyed goose
and talkin' all out the side of yo head"

she kept on talkin'
and her hair flitted wildly about in and out
of the rolled down window
I just ignored her
and her voice became distant to me

I drove into the black night down Highway 61

and suddenly, there it was … on the side of the road
just south of Clarksdale
in a field
just the other side of a barbed wire fence
just a standin' there lookin' at me as I drove past
and the damn thing spoke to me
somehow or another
it's voice was up inside my head

I must've startled girlie girl real good
'cause her ass came 'bout two feet off the seat
when I screamed real loud … to no one in particular
"what'd that fuckin' billy goat say!?"
"what fuckin' billy goat?" she screamed back at me
she was lookin' at me all wide-eyed like I was crazy

"that blue haired billy goat we passed back there"

girlie girl was silent for the first time
in a long time

I brought the truck to a skiddin', slidin' stop
and turned it around
and drove right back to where I saw that goat
and when I got there …
sure enough, there he still stood
just a chewin' … and chewin' … and chewin'
on some grass or somethin'

I got out of the truck
and walked right up the goat
and looked right at him
right square in his face
right up in his eyes

girlie girl was beside her drunk self
yellin' out the window

"heeeey, what the haaaill you dooooooin out thaaar'?"

the goat continued to chew
smackin' and droolin'
in a kinda circle like motion
so I asked him
"what did you say to me as I passed you by?"
the goat, in an indifferent manner, said,
"I am your karma"

"what!!!?, I asked … as I couldn't believe my ears
"I am your karma", the goat repeated
and he went back to chewin'
… payin' me never no mind

"well, I'll just be damned", I muttered
and turned to walk away'
I was certain I had lost my everlovin' mind
then, I clearly heard the goat say
"you must kill me and take me with you"

I turned around mighty sharply and said
"looky here mister talkin' goat
don't even tempt me …
with the mood I'm in
I might just take to slicin' your hairy throat
any minute now"
the goat said
"for I am your karma
you must do exactly as I say
it is just so"

girlie girl done got out of the truck and was staggerin'
on her way to where me and the goat was talkin'
her tits were just a bouncin'
like a country girl with no home trainin'

she stopped cold in her tracks
when she saw me
cut the throat of the billy goat
and her face turned as white as her ass is
where her panties cover it from the sun
when she goes to the creek to frolic around
with them other country people

I loaded the karma goat in the back of the truck
and got back in it ready to drive on … southbound

girlie girl wouldn't get back in

so, I left her drunk, country white ass just a standin' there
… 'side the road
I saw her in the sideview mirror … her mouth wide open …
in disbelief

me and karma goat headed on south
into the black night
towards Jackson

For Mary Frances

oh, beautiful lady …

you have caused others
who could not before
to hope once more

oh, gracious woman
you have given to so many
more than you had to give
selflessly

oh, kindest friend
you have been gentle
with hearts and souls
without just return of favor

oh reverent mother
you have provided nurturing breath
to precious children
and by it they live
and excel among millions
and they do so, mother …
because of you and for you

they will now utter words to you
that before they failed to speak
as you have taught them

oh, sweetest child of God
you have accomplished great things
and you remain to all
a model of golden goodness
… an image of incomparable humanity

~~ for Mary Frances King

Why You Never No More Smile?

little blessed sister looked directly into me
and sharply through me
so I looked back at her ... right into her

and I saw a curiosity
a question yet not answered
right there upon her face
she did not conceal it

little sister mused
and she looked away ... and returned
then away once more ... then again ... into me

the curiosity exploded and her mouth spit words
in the form of a question

"why you never no more smile?"
sweetly spoken

"I have no more smiles to give
not a single one
I ran completely out of smiles in the winter of '01
I want so very much to give you one
as you are without a smile of your own
and you, my young friend,
have use for many more smiles
I, though, do not

I never no more smile because I just cannot ...
but you ... my love ...
must forever smile"

Beneath the Bridge

as frozen ground is warmed
       by a punctual sun
as earth mist hazily rises
       skyward
as feathered creatures call
       for the morning to come
and ... as her futile search continues
       for remnants of my dark and distant heart
as these things occur ... I remain
       beneath the bridge

where I cannot be discovered
where I cannot be uncovered
where I will not be recovered

yet she maintains her lonely vigil
while those without hope have long since returned

... she sleeps not one moment
... she dreams no dream
... she smiles no smile
... and she will draw no further breath
until she has found me

though I remain
beneath the bridge

Reverend James and the Hampton Sisters

oh boy, the Reverend done gone and did it now
done made the congregation a big ol' promise
was the first thing he did when he got up there
'fore God and e'rybody
and confessed

boy, did he ever

ever once in a while … while he was 'fessin'
ol' Rev would peek out among 'em
through conjured up tears
just to see if they were believin' any of it
and when he knew he had 'em
right where he wanted 'em
he'd go to wailin'
like a lonely, mangy, hungry, lost dog

he'd cock his head back and look up into the ceilin'
and close his eyes
he'd belt it out .. he'd say "Jeeeeeeeezzuuuuusssss !!!"
and the church folks would say different things
but in the same kinda wailin' and moanin'

like

"praise the laawwd"   and
"hallelujah" and
"amen" and
"tell it" and
"preach it"

the Rev stretched his arms out
'bout as wide as they'd stretch
and he said

"Laaawwwdd … forgive me … please forgive my soul
I promise you, Lawd, if you'll let me get through this time
this trouble ..
this battle with none other than the most evil brother
Lucifer himself

if you will allow it, Lawd, I promise you,
whiskey won't ever touch these sweet lips again"

and another round of "tell it" and "amen" and "hallelujah"
and ol' Rev knew he had 'em

but no sooner than he thought it
a disturbance of sorts was happenin' in the back of the church
on the other side of the doors
and then them doors flung open
knocked Sister Lakeisha flat on her ass
and there come the Hampton sisters
Cloetta and Darvella
walkin' side to side ... swishin'
actin' like they couldn't see for the tears
wailin' and carryin' on
and they said

"Preacha .....

Preacha .... we knows you is a good man
but you done gone and did it now"

the Rev looked at Cloetta and then at Darvella
with his eyebriars all raised up on his farhead
he started to speak to the Hampton Sisters
that stood right there in front of him

but he was shut down
by one sharp wave of Darvella's hand

and she spoke ... softly at first

"Preacha ... Preacha ...
you sho' ought to be 'shamed of yoself
comin up in the house of the Lawd
and lookin' these good folk right in they eyes
and tellin' 'em you done stopped wit yo devil ways
.... 'cause you aint done nothin' of the such
it weren't but jist last night we done seen ya
we done seen ya down in the bottoms
right where you had no biness bein'

but you was there alright
you was there seein' our baby sister, Kenyetta
who aint yet turned sixteen
and don't even try to tell it like it was yo first time
'cause Kenyetta be carryin' yo child"

… and with that
… church was over
long before it was planned to be
the congregation was wailin' and moanin'
and callin' the Lawd
poor ol' Rev James let himself out the side door
and was never heard from again

Intermittent Monsters

she breathes softly onto my burdened shoulders
and with each exhalation sorrow escapes her withering soul
I can only silently weep with compassion
as her life ... in a whisper ... flows gently upon my skin

her chest rises and falls without rhythm
I can feel her disturbance
as she whimpers ... drowsily ... wearily

all I have to offer this child of angels ... is stillness
and solid presence

she deserves reward
she deserves decency
she desires resolution of dissonance
her mind craves peace

though the girl is regenerated by peaceful slumber
she wakes by intermittent monsters
and those creatures are the very ones that she loves
from there comes the conflict

she must first be burned to yearn ... it seems
she screams before she smiles
she must die to live

The Furry Stupids

they're all about me
damn critters
somber faced sour pusses
aint no good for nothin'
quite by god lucky they are
to be livin' in America
where they don't allow for skinnin'
and eatin' 'em
and they act like they know it
lookin' at me all the damn time
smug like
they're somewhat stupid
in my humble opinion
when they run out the door
to the outside world
aint long 'fore they want back in
and when the get back inside
they wantin' right back out again
… stupid, I say
they're furry
but they're quick
I can't catch 'em no matter how hard I try
it wouldn't be so bad
if there weren't so damn many of 'em
I'm all for neuterizin' and neutralizing them critters
so they can't breed willy nilly
then I wouldn't be surrounded
by the Furry Stupids

Brown Ballerina Box

it must have been missing
for a hundred years or more
until it was found by a curious boy
who had himself become lost
who had been nearly declared
to be with God in Heaven
assuming to have been delivered there
by a vessel of sinister death

but he was so alive
and he knew of no fear
for he had not known it before
boy and his naivety took it and held it
for eight hours into the sixth day

and when he was found
by the searching parties
of men with lights on their heads
that shown forward bright beams of light
that were dimmed slightly
by a slow creeping forest mist
and as they removed him from the sunken earth
he lost it
as mightily as he gripped it
as loudly as he protested
and as far as he could reach his bug-bitten
and bloodied arms
… he could not hold it
… he could not save it
… he could not bring it with him

forty-eight years removed
facing an inevitable digression
and the fate of immortality
he sought it and he found it … again
covered and concealed
by the progression of an evolving earth

he picked it up
as a gentle man would

and as delicately as he could
he opened it

by some force not of man
the plastic dancer made one revolution
only one
in pirouette pose
and was then … finally … still

he wept for her

Preservation

was whistling Dixie
walking and walking
toward no good place
toward no good end
gravel crunches beneath each step
and some ant head explodes
don't matter much too much
to the eco-balance of the world
then again … back then
Dixie was whistling
efforting to warn man
do not walk the gravel
for it is darkened by the blood
of no named black men
that traveled through a pass
… a pass where even the air was suspicious of them
bright evil eyes peered
from the rustling sage
and in a fury yet known to man
the slicing of throats commenced
and the blood stained the ground
and the hands of stately men
who from their lofty post
made it all about preservation

Mudhole

"I'll take her and throw her around, by damn"
he'd say at feeding time
when his hands were tied to the arms of the chair
"I'm gonna have that baby"
he'd say at bedtime
as if it were up for discussion or even possible
"damn!", he said to the man next door
"you sure are ugly ... half your damn face is caved in"
"now, now, Mudhole, hyperdown my toothless friend"
I would say to him
"my knees are hurting ... I can't, I can't, I can't make it"
he protested
"you're not walking, Mr. Mudhole, you're in your rolling chair
and I'm just behind you ... pushing"
"bye bye ...... bye darlin', bye"
he would mumble while waving to her ... someone
in his forever lost mind

on Sundays, when others had visitors of family
mainly sons and daughters, some grandchildren,
a few brothers and sisters and an occasional spouse
and they brought to them pies and stuff
and talked of things going on back home
on each and every Sunday ...when others would smile ...
Mudhole sat alone
and he rocked ... and muttered ... and drooled
he'd look left ... then right ... and try to look behind him
but just could see over his shoulders
because of the restraints
it was the fleeting moments of clarity that came about him
when he knew where and who he was
that I found wholly unbearable
like a caged animal

but the transparency of his eyes would be short lived
and the hazy glaze would soon return
and there he'd be ... again, on yet another Sunday afternoon
just a sittin', rockin', droolin, lookin' left, then right
alone
for Mudhole life lingered on and on and was no longer welcome

on occasion at night … when the quiet was nearly deafening
when creaking steps could be heard from a great distance
I could hear him … faintly
I could hear him
whispering words to her … someone
laying on his back, wrists bound to the rails
eyes wide open and staring at something … her …
far beyond the ceiling
and he spoke softly to her … partly unintelligible words
and I watched as but just once
he warmly smiled
a gummy smile … at her … I suppose
he'd say, with tears welling in the corners of his eyes
he'd say, "bye, bye … bye, bye darlin'
I'll see ya'll in the mudhole"

a month or more of Sundays came and went
and *The Death* had not yet visited upon Mudhole
though daily he prayed for a dark horse rider
with a lengthy blade
to pass by
and, in one swift fury … gut him

so, on an appropriate early Sunday morning
when the sun had not yet appeared
and the others slept in pharmaceutical peace
I gathered up Mudhole
and sat him in his rolling chair
and pushed him quietly down the hall
and our into the foggy morning
down the sidewalk, out across the grounds
and into the woods
there was no protest from him
just a sitti', rockin', mutterin' , droolin'
lookin' left, then right
through the trees to a crooked creek

"baby, I'm comin' to see ya", I recall him saying
"we're here, Mr. Mudhole", I said
and as sudden as it was ... it was over
he called to me but I could not look back
and as I ran ... as fast as I had ever

I heard him, though, yellin'
he'd say, "bye, bye ... bye, bye darlin'
I'll see ya'll in the mudhole"

In Elizabeth

tried to call you
from a Portuguese bar in Elizabeth
you did not answer
so I returned to her
and there we sat … her and I
upon our wisdom stools
remaining out of touch
with the entire sensation
the driver told me
there would be no one there
at
Le Bar Bat
and you were not there
where I wanted you to be
so I returned to her
and we talked
her about him
me about you
though there we were
upon our clouded minds
I had not yet seen such groovy grooving
by those starlit heartbreakers
the morning came too soon
and I was still in Elizabeth
you were not

I Cannot Remove You From My Eyes

as I cannot know you
as it is forbidden
as it haunts me
as I just sit here
across from you
so close
so far
I cannot remove you from my eyes
I do not have within me such strength
enough so that I may protect myself from you
though, it remains the truth
as it is soul melting
heart wrenching
yet entirely spellbinding
it must be to me
just out of reach
safe beyond my lure
you do, though, see me too
in a light no doubt dim
you do not see toothy smiles
but you certainly detect passion
… and an affectionate sense is about you
I wonder what you see … what you think … what you dream
what do you see in my eyes?
I cannot take them from you
I cannot remove you from them

Old Shack

old shack there
just there
old creaky and rotted wood shack
you sit just there
emerging from the morning mist

old shack of darkness
black evil spilling out and o'er
out of where there were once windows
o'er a threshold where stood a door
in a time before

old shack in the pine
you have stories
you are much like an old man

old shack keep them with you
keep your tales within
keep your secrets

the darkness is about you
it must not ... cannot be released

old shack there
no storm can destroy you
no winds can blow away your sinister history
no sunlight can illuminate your evil intent

old shack just there
remain just there
and harbor your mighty beasts

Oatmeal

oatmeal is good for the soul
comforting
I like oatmeal on the road
but not in bed
I like oatmeal … I said
if I were to share with you my oatmeal
I would put honey and berries in it
and give you a spoon
I might add pecans to them berries
or a sliced banana or two
… sautéed in butter
and if the oatmeal
got to be good to you
I would see no harm
if you tilted your bowl
and let the few tiny morsels that remained
fall slowly into your mouth
I make oatmeal with a little milk
my mother taught me how
her method by which
a proper serving
is to be mixed
during the course
of my many travels
I have always sought oatmeal
I do not take for granted
that I should find steel cut fare
so I bring along my own
to have with me there
home made for sure
instant surely sucks
oatmeal is grand … oatmeal is fine
but I have not yet tried
oatmeal with wine

~~ with Myrna Colley-Lee

Blonde Bartender Babe

told her with a straight drunken face
that I be a bull rider
she was no doubt impressed
and so was I
by my quite skillful and artful slinging of bullshit
tequila shots were on the house

Blonde Bartender Babe
... in the Houston
... of Texas

I wanted to marry her ... right then and there
I was Bobby Damn Delvechio
... from the Bronx
... of New York
by damn diddy damn damn
she could've easily been
Mrs. Blonde Damn Bartender Babe Delvechio
but I had to be on the way to the rodeo

Blonde Bartender Babe
... in Houston, Texas

Hippie Girl Happiness

Bohemian madness aside
Rastafarian nights considered
Caribbean smiles abundant

there is nothing that rivals
my hippie girl happiness

she is the best
better than the rest

sucking up delightful life
digesting carefree cookie clouds
and a ginseng mocha cocktail

death to all armpit shavers
she hasn't bathed for six glorious days

God bless … won't ya please
… my hippie girl happiness

smokin' weed and plantin' seed
hope we have a sack full of granola eatin' youngens

I'm a procreatin', regneratin', ovulatin' lusty slug

but

my hippie girl happiness loves me
that's all that matters

Coast of Impossible Waters

pulled an all-nighter
on the Coast of Impossible Waters
woke up some afternoon thereafter
beside a blonde-ish girl
from the University of Anywhere
she was not astonished
by our tangled mess of limbs

God broke her down on Highway 49
near a Pentecostal Church of Contradiction
the wind of whiskey in my sails
I swooped down on her
and brought her there to safe harbor
where we made a mockery of love
… and no sense of it at all

but soon enough
she went rapidly on to leave me
beneath a cloud of guilty calm
and there I have since remained

only but only a memory or a few
saves me from clawing myself bloodless
up inside Boneshakers in the Houston of Texas
I felt a soul-shaking sensation
as Latasha … with dark brown eyes
discreetly rubbed my inner mind
'cause James and another James
damn sho' would not have approved

then … in the Neshoba County night
by a perfect lamplight
she came only to kiss me
thus killing me by method of amplified pleasure
there upon the blue path of righteousness
somewhere between Memphis
and the Gulf of Corporate Toxin
I stumbled upon The Madness
and her name was Providence

she took me by my scarred and weathered hand
and certainly I did follow
we veered far off course
and the moon soon found us
illuminating our indiscretions
and revealing monumental passion
at the edge of best intentions
I could only feel her
as mostly common people
were in attendance
of our happy moment

and there were colors over our heads
that rivaled the splendor of rainbows

took a long drive to Beaumont
with her seated crosslegged
beside me …
and she still visits me
on dark and lonely nights
when I need her most

Burned and Blowed Up Children

Addie Mae, Cynthia, Carol and little Denise
went to church
on an otherwise indifferent Sunday morning
on the 15th of September
the year of our Lord, 1963

and there in the house of God
beneath a proper blue but deceptive sky
and an ill-assumed perception
... of glorious and joyful shelter

there
beneath a holy construction
while gathered in praise
they were blowed apart and burned to a screaming death
for a good enough reason
... 'cause some somebody didn't care too much for black folk

so little Addie Mae was born having dark skin
and she had no say in it

and precious Cynthia was born a black girl
and nobody asked her if she preferred to be different

and sweet, sweet Carol was born a negro
and she never thought anything of it

and the youngest angel, Denise
who smiled as radiantly as any sun
... and did not know of a difference
... in the colors
... of the skin of men
was born unto niggers
and for that her tiny body
was blowed to bloody pieces

and then there was silence

for many years … silence

not a word from those that carried with them justice
not a word from those that held the truth

silence … …. …

 even God was silent

Truth Meadows

would you smile for my life
if that was all I wanted?
if that was all I needed?
would you live a while longer
if I could convince you to?
if I could tell you why you should?
would you not flee from me at rapid pace?
if I could only show you
if I could reveal to you the truth
If I could cause you to see
… the beauty of you
if I could slow you down
and stand you at the edge of a reflective brook?
would you follow me?
would you walk along beside me?
would you go with me there?
would you hold on to me
and you let me carry you
to where you are welcome?
would you come with me
and no longer tremble
to a place where dreams are allowed?
could you be not with tears
so that you could see
what is before you?
... in the Truth Meadows
would you now smile for me?
because that is all I want
that is all I need

As Go Fairies Go I

I follow them
stooping at times
to pass beneath a bridge
brick bridge over my head
cursed creek splits my feet
what is there beyond the brush?
way on beyond my jaded perception
where there dwells but no sensitivity
there is among men
a hesitation
... and so I do not follow men
yet
as go fairies go I
so I follow them
lurking a times
in the shade of shadows
shadowy shade conceals my apathetic eyes
what is there beyond the truth?
a great distance beyond my imagination
where there may exist God
there is about men
a reservation
... thus I do not follow men
yet
as go fairies go I
so I follow them
hiding at times
in hollow reality
to avoid being pelted by indignant daggers
what is there beyond humanity?
a deep and despairing chasm
whereupon all men fall

there is about men
a lifelessness
... and so I do not follow men
yet
as go fairies go I

The Sun Came Out For You Today

the sun came out for you today
... and because of you

you have wept beneath cold and gray skies
for far too many days

rained and stormed upon your vulnerable soul
... exposed

pelted and pounded
by unrelenting bolts of self-loathing lightning
from horrid heavens of despair

you have been bathed in blue pity
and wearing an ashen face
since that day

you have lost your smile

... but

the sun came out for you today
... and because of you

Worm Man

when I was young
my dad took me fishing
at four by God thirty
in the pitch black morning
we never went straight to the lake
we always had to stop
and get fishing bait
to catch the fish, of course
and my dad would ask me
if I would like some "nicky nacks"
("nicky nacks" = snacks)
you bet I would
cheese 'n crackers
they were called "nabs"
but they were in the nicky nack family
of snacks
maybe a pickled egg
or two
a Barqs root beer
and quite possibly
a can of mustard sardines

and then my dad would speak to an old wrinkled man
seated at a table
sipping coffee from a cup
wearing a white-ish shirt
stained on the front
by missed sips of coffee

"we'll take a box of them nightcrawlers, sir"
my dad would say
and the wrinkled man
would slowly turn
while remaining seated
and reach into a beat up ol' ice chest
and turn and give the box to my dad
my dad would give the man
a solid dollar
and the man gave my dad
some sum of change

oh I'd ask about the man
as we drove from darkness into the dawn of the day

"what is that man's name?"
"how did he get all wrinkled?"
"why does he look so sad?"
"where does he live?"
"does he have a mom and dad?"
"does he have any friends?"

never got a straight forward answer
from my dad
about the wrinkled man
he might would say
"boy, you sure do ask a lot of questions"

and at that
 I'd remain quiet
and fish
and try not to tangle my line in a tree limb
but … on the way home
usually in silence
I'd say to my dad
"I don't want to be like the wrinkled old Worm Man"

My Mother Loved Gardenias

my mother loved Gardenias
and White Shoulders perfume
and Vicksburg
and her comfortable couch
... conformed just so
she liked to read books about people
because she liked people
she liked Mexican food
and picking blackberries
and driving to Port Isabel
she loved a son she never held
and would never know
she liked Archie ... thus ... Ole Miss
she was fond of New Augusta
and Aunt Judy
and Rayford Waldrop
and Aunt Kat
my mother loved the ocean
and the waves
and the sea spray
and sea shells
my mother loved life
but
while I was at the ocean
enjoying the waves
the sea spray
the sea shells
and life

... she died

Pills All Day

I'm a walkin' talkin' wreck
an emotional tilt-a-whirl
a blended fruit drink of sensitivities
just an overall frayed tangle of nerves

pills all day
I take 'em 'til I feel better

a basket case for sure
speakin' gibberty jabber
and makin' no sense
to anyone at all

so gimme them pills all day
'til the night takes me away

my juices all tastin'
bitter and off
got my skin crawlin'
with tiny itchin' creatures

let me have my bottle of pills
let me kill one or the other of us

I take pills all day
I'm not so happy to say
I take pills all day
just so I can say, "hey"
… to you

The Brought Low

on some ... but ... too few
sleepless nights
that ... sooner than I am aware
turns to still yet dark morning
and the tired stars fill my window

on these fair and good occasions
when it occurs
a slight and gentle breeze will
quite discreetly ... grace my face
and bring along a fragrance
a fragrance of her
... undeniably her

and I am brought low
by a reminiscent flow
of a lifeblood
lost long ago

I am brought low
for I know
it is merely an olfactory illusion
spiritual at best
yet, she remains, for me ... vanished

I am thankful ... for certain
to the gods of dreams and apparitions
and if it were to become
a matter of doubt and question
I would and surely could
for a thousand years
hold my eyes wide open
and not slumber
a single fraction of any second
for it might be the very instant
she is brought to me again
on such an infrequent slow wind
of forgotten happiness

yes, I will be brought low ... again
though I will know
but not until and only then
that I have lived

The Kitchen Floor

I ate from the kitchen floor last tonight
because I could not raise myself
to be level with decency

I waited
as though a rat would
just inside of my designated quarters
when the Normals
had retired
and were dreaming of things not me
I made my way ...
slowly and carefully
toward the kitchen
and when I stepped into
this place of pleasant sustenance
I was brought low by a force familiar

down to my knees and onto the floor
I was not surprised ... I was not startled
I had been there before ... on the kitchen floor
I thought of things while there
as I could not do much more
and I deserved no less
like an insidious sore
I'd become a mess
an infectious mess galore

the Normals should not suffer
for my afflictions
they should be revered
and held in high esteem
for they have done as much
... as they can do
far more than I deserve

be that as it may
I laid prone for a while and thought
there has to be to life
much, much more
than this cold, cold ... kitchen floor

By a Far Moon I See

by an illuminating memory
I can see
the place
from where I've come
and I go there
in return
and there ... once there
I notice
the old school is smaller
the hallways are darker
the sun shines less radiant
the streets
... by which I traveled ... to and fro upon
... and onward toward uncertainty
are now greatly worn
the paint
on city buildings
has faded
the people are weathered
exuberance diminished
I see not dawn
but rather dusk
yet I am home
and though I fled
it did not leave me
thus it is so
wherever I find me to be
it is on such clear nights
when the parade of clouds
slow and part
so that by a far moon I can see
the youth of me

~~ with Jennifer Crain Aitken

New Augusta

New Augusta here I come
ridin' proud down 98 Highway
(in the backseat of Pop's silver Catalina)
take me there … take me there … get me there now

ever anxious to roll them spools
right through the middle of town
watch out Miss Hannah Cooper
if'n I get the country nerve
I'm a gonna … I'm a gonna … I'm a gonna make you mine
I don't know what I'll do with ya but you sho is pretty
Edwin Patterson ain't got nothin' on me
I'll knock him a new one
and sport you around to all my summer friends

we goin' campin'
behind the old Thomas place
me and Jimbo and Tony and Ricky
"them cows aint gonna get us will they?"
I'll be damned if they didn't … they got us good

got us in an awkward situation … fer sure

and there but for Jimbo
I would have certainly been gored

oh, New Augusta

Sack of Smiles

all I have for them
is a big ol' sack of smiles
brilliant … radiant … sparkling

reach my bloody hand
into my sick sack of smiles
worming … squirming … sloppy slurping

resisting attachment like crazy babies
I can't get one to stick
on my static face

all I have for them
is a sack of smiles
… where I put them when I could not

I've saved them all
put them away one by one
and now I have a wrinkled sack full of smiles

Celebratory Dreamy Reunification

dreamy … dreamy … dreamy
    I still dream of you

you moaned amid your fitful slumber
you did call my name
… you called me inward
… you called me forth

I became your fighter
I became your cause
and though now you rebuke me
I am still caused by you

did I see you walking by as slowly as you cared?
and did I see you pass me (at the intersection of my life)?

and though you will not admit it
did I notice your eyes cut to me?
did I feel the way I did or was it merely some lost longing?

did you avoid my return by curt dismissal?
were you not prepared for what you truly desired?
were you not enthralled by us at all?

The Beauty of Bombs

aside from the economy of it all
it makes perfect bloody sense
to drop death from the skies
toward which children have … for eternity
… gazed curiously
and while wondering … where is this god?

such blue and cotton heavens cannot be but good
such sun … then at night … moonglow
can be none other than lasting tranquility
and … hideously … as much as children caress our souls
we blow 'em up for little or nothing
that is the beauty of bombs

for their father's transgressions
and for the sake of national insecurity
and for redemption
we must detach their head from shoulders
by way of scorching heat and twisted metal
indiscriminate carnage … collateral damage
that is the beauty of bombs

and though we proclaim righteousness
while living in the shadows of shame
we are yet killers of children and thus wholly unworthy
of any such Christian mercy at all
… blow 'em up … sweep 'em up …
incinerate the tiny parts
and inhale the bone dust

oh, the beauty of bombs

Providence and the Diminutive Man

there before I on a Monday afternoon
was Providence
her vulnerabilities exposed
and she led me to forever
which was wherever
we could be found together
… Providence and I

I am now nothing more than a diminutive man
I was formerly somebody
now I am someone I'm not
a ghost of me
uncharacteristically forgotten
by the family I've failed but always loved
... thus, there is yet Providence

she is increasingly by my side
I am beside myself
she guides … I glide
and if Providence weren't enough
her sister, Salvation, is ever ready
to keep The Death at bay
thus there is Providence then Salvation

though I remain but a diminutive man
I am forgiven by the unforgiven
and so I go confidently
toward my misfortune
Providence leads me there … by hoop in nostril
Salvation awaits me there
… without judgement

Thing

way, way on down the tracks
'bout nearly a mile or more
far, much farther than a seein' man can see
there is a thing down there
a thing I cannot see
but I know it is there
'cause I sense this thing
I feel this thing in my blood and in my bones
it chills me right through my skin
and as deep as to my soul
way on down them tracks
where no walkin' man dare go
but have mercy on me
I am called and lured to this thing
way on down the tracks
and 'round a haunting bend
and through a knee-high devil's mist
though I cannot see thing that has me
I feel it is *The Death*
and ... on each journey there
as I step ever closer to it
I become more at peace
and soon The *Death* does not shiver me
it is merely a thing
way, way on down the tracks
toward great uncertainty

Every Quarter Moon

she would see me
she would come to me
once beneath every quarter moon
in a field of tall grass
caused to brush and make tranquil sound
… and soothe fair gods
by a warm wind unhurried

and all she wanted to do
was lay her weary head upon me
not for a minute … but for hours
I allowed her to

and she would remark of the stars
and their chaotic placement
she would assure me
that there be among them … a message
a message from her god to us

so on those nights
she would sweetly ask me
to seek this message
and speak to her
in a whisper
… speak to her
whatever meaning I should discover

I would do that
and tell her
to sleep without worry
slumber in peace … rather
… with good dreams

~~ with Haley S. Bowman

Vanished Son

on a day
not remembered
in a place
no longer found
in a rain
from no apparent cloud
... above

a first and yet only son
was born
unto her
though not for her

and he was taken
then given
into folded hands

a door silently opened
then slammed loudly shut

and this son of the union of an unknown son
and a daughter of an immoral moon
was then vanished
into a great and volatile sea
of humanity

on another day
a day to be remembered
in a place with a happy name
and in no rain
a second son
was born into the light
given by a merciful sun

and he was kept
and raised to be righteous

so it was
for nearly a lifetime

then
in a rain
and
in the mind
of the second son
the first
came to be

so on a path
he set
to seek
the first son
and unknown brother

and he did find him

Her Great Indulgence

as I am weary
and filthy
and shot below the belt
by a low riding thug
having as his good fortune
only one bullet remaining
and … bitch luck

I am done
completely so
for I cannot finish
for I haven't a mount
and not enough blood
to beat my hollow and sickened heart

so I lay with the dirt
and dream by the stars
and on the canvass
of some brilliant moons
I watched as the person who is me
though I am here
wasted a good life

I reflect
being born of peasant unification
and knowing now
that such birth
is living death

so I was left with no remedy
I called out for her
to come to me
from her place majestic

she is the Blessed Magnificence
and if it were to be
that she could reach me
I'd rather die
of her great indulgence

Bad Dreamin' ... Again

went to the candy store
bought me some candy
made me feel dandy

walked on down to the bank of the River Reflection
peered over to the other side
saw a boy
over there
on the other side
looked about like me
he chewed on some candy too

waved at the boy that looked about like me
he waved right back
and grinned a bit of a grin
so I grinned too
then he was gone

walked to the center of town
stopped in front of the haircuttin' shop
man sat in as chair
holding a newspaper
saw the front page
it read
"Boy Drowns in River Reflection While Eating Candy and
  Grinning"

made me sad
real bad sad
hurried so fast
ran to my only mother
she hugged me real tight
cried 'til I slept
woke up in her arms
asked my only mother
she said I'd been Bad Dreamin' ...

Hollow Branch

I am a branch
fallen
from a grand oak
by a brooks bend
hollow is the branch
that is me
hollow is my heart
so I float
as empty people do
from one love to the other
by a current chaotic
I go forth
at great speed
and little effort
until
I will some day
arrive at rest
in life, love or death

~~ with Whitley G. Miller

For Eyes Gone Blind and Hearts Grown Cold

on the frozen earth I laid still
... entirely motionless

and a dark mare came forth
... stomping and shaking the ground beneath me
... spraying snot from her flared nostrils
... and sensing my odor present

upon the mare sat the master of my existence
... with eyes that caused all others to bow upon bended knees

though I laid with the god of calm
... I trembled, nonetheless, in horror

the cold wind blew
... upon my blistered skin
... and peeled it back
... exposing my tender spirit
... yielding my emotive self

the dark horse rider passed me by
and, for the moment, the inevitable was delayed
but imminent arrival was certain

The Death came suddenly and hurriedly for me
... advancing at a pace I could not sustain
... I ran ... then, with childish and innocent fear
... as if toward my mother's outstretched arms
... yet she was just beyond my reach

as I recalled affection
... as distant as it was
... I remembered her
... as distant as she was

and *The Death* certainly caught me
... and turned slowly with my body enmeshed
... between its bloody teeth
... and it was in this fashion that *The Death* and I
... soon arrived at Hell's Gate

The Death was consumed me
… causing me to repent
… begging for forgiveness
… so, I closed my eyes and died

now I am a hollow man
soulless through and through
I spit in the face of compassion
and mate with astounding indifference

The Chair

stained wood beneath cotton skies
unnoticed, unprotected, unresolved

there sits the chair
that no longer rocks
... except on blustery nights
when rain is forthcoming

lonely, lonely inanimate object
that harbors no memories
and hears no more
of the conversations of the morose ones
that once occupied the chair

creatures, like birds, sometimes perch upon the arms
but quickly become dispassionate about the whole affair
and fly far ... far away ... from the chair

so the chair
sits just there ... lacking emotion
without the companionship of humanity

once ...

a boy was lovingly rocked to sleep in his mother's arms
... in the chair
a woman read a letter from a son at war
... while seated in the chair
a son proposed marriage to a beautiful young woman
... as she sat in the chair
a man wept uncontrollably over the loss of a father
... in the chair
and
a thousand or more times someone said "I love you"
... as they sat in the chair

and now ...

there is a silence about the chair
a solitude

a lonely demeanor

this chair
this chair that sits just there
has ... through countless years
and immeasurable tears ...
absorbed life

and now
minute by blistering minute
the gentle winds
cause the memories to rise in dissipation
as a whisper would
and slowly become forgotten

out there sits the chair
where life has occurred

Precious and Simplicity

in her mind there exists an urgency of companionship
there resides a necessity for nurturing
… in her mind
she conceals her vulnerabilities exceptionally well
she reveals her beauty without reservation

her name is Precious and she was born of simplicity

times were damned awful then
we all suffered greatly
no quarter granted to friend or foe
she emerged unscathed
from the twisted rubble of a world imploding

her name is Precious and she was born of simplicity

in her mind there dwells a glut of secluded yearning
in her eyes there is rampant anticipation
she holds her obsession in the palms of her hands
she embraces my desire in her heart

her name is Precious and she was born of simplicity

Mind Smile

he blows life into his Hohner
slickly slices through
the dark, oppressive nothing
that is a delta night
black man don't like no haints
I don't either
black man don't like no dead people
neither do I
black man gots him some soul
so do I
black man wants to live in peace
don't we all?
black man wants himself a fair chance
it should be so
black man's blood be red
as red as my own
black man's heart beats by passion of a woman
so does mine
black man wants justice
just as we all do
black man wants definite dignity
yes
he draws a great and painful inhalation
of an air cleansed by the filter of struggle
and if such things could be seen
all present would have surely observed
his great big mind smile

~~ with John A. Walls

2,742 Blackbirds

sounded like the end of the world
when they flew over top my head
scared me skinny
liked I knowed I was
'bout to be dead
if it did happen to happen
that they killeded me
just by skeerin' me white
then I'll just be doomed and damned
  … and dead
but they didn't killeded me narn at all
they just flew right on by
probably headed north
to scare the hairs right off the head
of some 'nother boy
out walkin' … just a mindin' his own business
anyways …
they was gone
all 2,742 of them blackbirds
they was gone

Sick House

I dreamed of you
in my darkness
I dreamed ... of you
and that is where we met
... in my darkness

beyond rotten fallen fences
across barren fields
where nothing grows from haunted soil
where a madness lingers ... as a fog
there is where I find you
... in my darkness

beneath gray tone skies
and far below any sun of man
where no one should be found
where there is not vision
there is where I meet you
... in my hollow heart

behind steel wicked doors
and down haunted hallways
where God will not visit
where *The Death* remains
there is where I feel you
... behind me
... in my breathlessness
there ... in that sick house ... is the fear
there ... among the unwell ... is the horror
along a broken footbridge I walk
without concern
without trepidation
toward infected monsters

along a trail of defeated spirits
toward a bed of resignation
this is where I will lay with you
in the godforeverdamned sick house

Drunk in the Morning

when me and Baby was hangin'
peoples didn't understand
they just looked at us
like we done come from some 'nother planet
or somewheres not from 'round here
lookin' at us like we had the sense of an acorn
like was from way out in the country

well … I gots news for 'em
they aint got no dad gum business
passin' a judgin' on some somebodies
of the likes of me and Baby

just 'cause we didn't go real regular like
to the house of education
which is why we works at night
'cause we can't get no day time, regular like jobs
just 'cause we don't drive no fancy-stylin' car
and just 'cause Baby done give birth to a youngen'
'fore she turned 16
(I love that little crumbsnatching fella
like he was my own blood related)

just 'cause me and Baby talk kinda funny
and Baby can't help it if she looks a little funny
… in a cute kinda way
I'd a never noticed it
had my friend, DeWayne not told me 'bout it
'bout one of her teats was bigger than the otherin'
it didn't really bother me 'cause Baby loves me
just how I am
"ain't no body perfect", she'd say
and I always believed her 'bout that

so them folks looked at us sideways
all they wanted to
I didn't care none-at-all
they stared and sneered
all they wanted to
me and Baby still did our thing

we got off our jobs at six in the mornin'
and we drank cold beers
'cause there weren't nothin' like
bein' drunk in the mornin'

I loved Baby and she loved me
but sometimes I'd lay in bed at night
and my mind would go to wanderin' and wonderin'
just how ol' DeWayne knowed
'bout how Baby's teats be lopsided

Of Morpheus

descend me amid the fog of apathy
down winding path toward a foothill village
tread me upon memorable earth
and go I forth to wanting warmth
be I distant from her
be I desirous
be that I long for her soothing touch
and thus I walk
toward the death of my demons
… toward my sister salvation
where she waits
at all trails end
and there I am received
without such judgment
and less indignation
she merely holds me
and in quiet concert I release
there I am found
breath upon bosom
and *The Death* turned away
yet certainly to return
though not on this day

~~ with T. Hollingsworth

Ancient Tree

ancient tree
sit there beneath winter heartbreak
and be burdened by the contravention of man

tree of immeasurable wisdom
limbs be weighted and deadened

decay will set from outward in

and time is not kind
all things end
old trees become then fallen

upon forest floors they rot
into the earth
without decent notice

and then ... in some time
they are forgotten
ancient trees
much like men

yet from men escape souls
and in spiracle waft they go
... the souls of men

but trees
being soulless
have earthly bindings

so upon cold forest ground
they rot
ancient trees

She Called Me Fucker

once she bought and brought to me a giant cookie
from the giant cookie gettin' store
she instructed the giant cookie salesperson
to write upon it
      (in tasty white icing)

      "Happy Birthday Fucker"

she presented the giant and obscene cookie to me
I was impressed and quite moved
by the gesture

she'd call me on the phone
and her loving and affectionate greeting would always be:

      "hey Fucker"

I fell head over heels for this foul mouth princess
and I would have loved her 'til the end of time
but, alas
she went and met another fucker

Old Clock

old clock on the wall
reads 3:09
doesn't indicate am or pm
not that kind of clock
nevertheless, it is wrong
hasn't been right
in so very long
no longer matters

old clock on the wall
there ... over there
on that far away wall
is wrong
but still tics
... and tocs
though in labored manner

old clock on the wall
much like me
humbly efforts to see

old clock on the wall
much like me
simply struggles to be

may not be
too distant in time
from this countable moment
when the old
and formerly useful
and indifferent
clock
tics
a final toc

though much like me
old clock on the wall
does not abruptly stop
old clock on the wall
just winds its way down
unnoticeably
into oblivion
much like me

~~ with Connie Wren

Zeppelinfeld (1985)

we remained too quiet
on the overnight train to Nurnberg
and when we arrived at 3 am
we went to the home of her friends
somewhere in the city
they weren't really her friends at all
I could not be angry at her
but only for a brief moment
she did not allow me to sour my face for long
18 and happy cannot be defeated
we went to a concert on Saturday
Deep Purple at Zeppelinfeld
I stood where Hitler once stood and spoke

she took good care of me
me and her amid 75 thousand
we were oblivious
she may have loved me ... I could not know
she was my first ever hippie girl
and I was but a government mule

later she came to Vilseck
and brought me mail from home
we took in a movie
she laughed heartily
at what I did not know
so I laughed in return … at her

we crossed a bridge over water
that split the city
then our time was over but not complete
we remained too quiet
on the overnight train …
to the remainder of my life

Mirror

mirror ... tell me only the truth
be not deceptive to me
be not less than honest
... in your reflection

reveal to me
who I am
... and why

do not be subtle
do not be kind

simply illuminate me
and expose me

do not be dim
do not be hazy
do not be cloudy
be as clear as diamonds

if you, my mirror, are no less approving
then I shall be at ease

if you, my mirror, reflect the horror of what I am
then it shall be confirmed

I am what I appear to be

Big Pop Wouldn't Let 'em In

Big Pop wouldn't let 'em in
made 'em go 'round back

I seen them big ol' nigger man's eyes
starin' through the screen door
tryin' to ask for help
two black sweatin' nigger boys
stood right by him
barely tall enough to be 'bove his knees

Big Pop wouldn't let 'em in
made 'em go 'round back

dirty faced black man begged
for the life of his black wife
said she was sleepin' sick side the road
couple miles away down highway 98
big ol' tears ran down
his black and weathered face
and his voice cracked with fear

Big Pop wouldn't let 'em in
made 'em go 'round back

black man's boys stared
through the screen of the door
with a nothingness behind them eyes
I seen them nigger boys lookin' right at me
waiting on the mercy
they had yet to know
little boys ... just little boys
like me

Big Pop wouldn't let 'em in
made 'em go 'round back

black man turned slow and walked away
black boys in tow
I watched them go

one black boy turned and looked back at me
his sad eyes pleading and wondering
… why?

and they traveled onward
south on highway 98

Big Pop wouldn't let 'em in
made 'em go 'round back

Big Pop watched them as they walked away
heads hung low
and soon they could not be seen
the road consumed them

"storms comin'", Big Pop said
"them niggers gonna get soaked"

I could see in his eyes a sadness
a troubling
"yes, sir", I said
"and they aint got them no raincoats"

and my thoughts quickly turned to playin'
and candy and root beers and such
I tried not to worry 'bout them niggers no more
the customers came and went
and the highway sounds were steady
I was happy on my face
but sad in my heart

Big Pop wouldn't let 'em in
made 'em go 'round back

Big Pop kept lookin' down the road
in the way that they went

"what ya' thinkin' 'bout Big Pop?" … I asked
"thinkin' 'bout them niggers" … he said
"what about 'em, Big Pop?"
"they gonna get mighty wet in that storm" … he mumbled
"rain ain't gonna melt them niggers" … I said

"but if their mama dies …
that sure is gonna make them boys sad"

Big Pop wouldn't let 'em in
made 'em go 'round back

Big Pop went back to tending to cars
and oil and windshields and such
but I could tell
his mind was on them niggers that came for help
the way he kept stoppin' and lookin' down the highway
in the way that they went

the storms came and the rain fell hard
we went inside … me and my Big Pop
I looked at him
and saw the sadness was even more than before
I sat in his lap and said to him
"don't go worryin' yourself too much, Big Pop
… God will take care of them niggers …
God don't care what color they are"

Big Pop wouldn't let 'em in
made 'em go 'round back

"get yo jacket, boy"
Big Pop said to me
and I did just that
we jumped in the truck and away we went
south on highway 98
in the way that they went
we drove through the rain and the wind
barely could see
'til we found them niggers … broke down
right where they said they'd be

as we got closer I could see them boys faces
lookin' out the back of the truck
… wide eyed … scared

Big Pop wouldn't let 'em in
made 'em go 'round back

Big Pop loaded them niggers in the truck
even the sick mama
the black man helped Big Pop put her in the truck
we drove back to the cafe and Big Pop told us to go in
"all of us?" I asked
he looked at me like he did sometimes
and I knew the answer

and to the surprise of all that were present
we walked right up inside the café … me and them niggers
right up among the white folk

and there were looks of shock and contempt
someone yelled out to my Big Pop,
"Bill, what ya lettin' them niggers in here for?"
Big Pop paid him never no mind

Big Pop wouldn't let 'em in
made 'em go 'round back

Big Pop sped away in his truck
with the black boys mama laid 'cross his seat
her head in his lap and her eyes closed shut

Big Pop hurried and drove real fast
to the hospital 'bout thirty miles away
when he got there he called out for help

when them white doctors and nurses saw that Big Pop
was helping a negro out of the truck and tryin' to bring her up in
the hospital – they kinda frowned at him

and they regretted they did
Big Pop told them nurses and doctors
what was gonna be what
and she was taken in
and she did not die
… on account of my Big Pop

Big Pop wouldn't let 'em in
made 'em go 'round back

and the story was told
all about the town
'bout how Big Pop helped them niggers that day
and he was either hated or loved for it
didn't matter much whichever to my Big Pop
he just went about his business
as if the world were never no different
I knew, though, that somehow it had changed

Big Pop wouldn't let 'em in
made 'em go 'round back

years passed
and *The Death* came to visit upon Big Pop

and on the day he was to be buried
many good people came from all over
and brought food and flowers and such

Big Pop was there but gone
in that old pine box

them boys came with their father
and their mother came too
the one that lives on account of my Big Pop

the boys had grown into men and their father was old
lots of other black folk were there too

Big Pop wouldn't let 'em in
made 'em go 'round back

when all who came to pay their respects to Big Pop
had come and gone
I saw that old black man go into the room
where Big Pop was just a laying there cold
in that old pine box
and the old black man ... with hat in hand ... slowly walked up to
my Big Pop
and stood there and stared at him for a long time
then he reached out his black and weathered hand
tremblin' ... shakin'

and put it gently on Big Pop's face …
… for a minute or two
and that old black man leaned over and whispered
in my Big Pop's ear
what, I could not hear
I know my Big Pop heard him though

old black man turned and walked away
had big ol' tears rolling down his face again

Big Pop wouldn't let 'em in
made 'em go 'round back

Flower Child Sparrow Farrow

ol' girl had a child
said the baby reminded her of tulips
so she named her Flower
Flower Child Farrow
later someone added … for amusement … the name of a bird
on account of how she pursed her lips at feeding time
so it became Flower Child Sparrow Farrow
and remained so for as long as she drew breath
which turned out to be just 11 days shy of 17 years
Flower bloomed much too soon
and before she knew better of it
the nail was in her
and the sickness settled in
and there was nothing anyone could
or would do
for Flower Child Sparrow Farrow
except watch her wilt

Until I Saw You

I've seen the mystical mountains
with tops penetrating the softness of clouds
peaking just above the floor of Heaven
and it was then
the most beautiful sight my eyes had seen

I've watched a majestic bird with wings the span of time
glide effortlessly above the greenest forest
and deepest bluest smoothest reflective lake
and it was then
the most beautiful sight my eyes had seen

I've observed the birth of a child
and the indescribable love on the face of the new mother
as tears were dried and she looked into the eyes of a son
and it was then
the most beautiful sight my eyes had seen

I've seen animals save animals and men save men
and animals and men save one another
and it was then
the most beautiful sight my eyes had seen
I've seen the Northern Lights
and the Southern Cross
the Eastern Star
and the Western Hills

I've watched men go to God
in vessels driven by *The Death*
and be welcomed by open-winged angels
and brought in with no more to suffer

I've seen these magnificent and wonderful things
and they were then
the most beautiful things I had ever seen

… until I saw you

Six Mile Road

what is at the end of this path?
I've been told it was an old road
... an old road I'm told

what winds have blown 'cross this road?
I've been told that they were harsh winds
... harsh winds I'm told

what spirits were among the tops of pines along this road
I've been told that they were the most nefarious of spirits
... concertedly wicked I'm told

what of the fate of men that traveled this road?
I've been told not to speak of such fate
... unspeakable I'm told

what of the souls of men that traversed this passage?
I've been told that they had none
... soulless I'm told

so ... I go myself
... I shall begin at end of civilization
... where goodness abruptly stops and evil subtly seduces
... and travel forward ever cautious
... toward the hideousness of humanity
... thru the treacherous darkness of man's path
... where there is great fear of unknown things
... and no weakness unrevealed

and on and further on
thru to the end of the Six Mile Road
where from yet no man has yet emerged

for I cannot resist the greatest of human temptation
... to best fellow men
... to conquer the not yet conquered
... to endure the intolerable
... to survive the godawful
... to defy The Evil

though I proved victorious
and though I did slay demon dragons
and persevered mighty sufferings
to emerge outwardly unscathed
I am not ever again the same
and will be eternally at the mercy of
… the Six Mile Road

AUTHOR BIOGRAPHY

Thomas R. Ruffin was born on February 22, 1963 in Hattiesburg, Mississippi.

Thomas studied at Central Texas College, The University of Southern Mississippi, Rutgers University and Mississippi College where he received his Bachelor of Science and Master of Social Sciences degrees. Thomas also taught at Mississippi College (Department of History and Political Science). Thomas resides in Clinton, Mississippi.

For more information about Thomas R. Ruffin visit:

http://ruffinonline.wixsite.com/ruffinonline

CONTRIBUTORS (in order of appearance)

Cover Illustration	Steve Cash
Inside Illustration	Steve Cash
"The Precious Indignity"	with Jana Barlow Feldman
"Death in Cotton"	with Myrna Colley-Lee
"Oatmeal"	with Myrna Colley-Lee
"By a Far Moon I See"	with Jennifer Crain Aitken
"Every Quarter Moon"	with Haley S. Bowman
"Hollow Branch"	with Whitley G. Miller
"Mind Smile"	with John A. Walls
"Of Morpheus"	with T. Hollingsworth
"Old Clock"	with Connie Wren
Back Cover Photo	Nikki Hall

Made in the USA
Charleston, SC
17 October 2016